Text processing

20 Cambridge Computer Science Texts

Text processing

A. Colin Day

Computer Centre, University College London

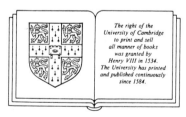

The right of the
University of Cambridge
to print and sell
all manner of books
was granted by
Henry VIII in 1534.
The University has printed
and published continuously
since 1584.

Cambridge University Press

CAMBRIDGE

LONDON   NEW YORK   NEW ROCHELLE

MELBOURNE   SYDNEY

Published by the Press Syndicate of the University of Cambridge
The Pitt Building, Trumpington Street, Cambridge CB2 1RP
32 East 57th Street, New York, NY 10022, USA
296 Beaconsfield Parade, Middle Park, Melbourne 3206, Australia

First published 1984

Printed in Great Britain at the University Press, Cambridge

Library of Congress catalogue card number:

British Library cataloguing in publication data
Day, A. Colin
Text processing — (Cambridge computer science texts; 20)
1. Information storage and retrieval systems
I. Title
001.64   Z699.3

ISBN 0 521 24432 3 hard covers
ISBN 0 521 28683 2 paperback

Contents

Preface

In the early days of computers it was common to regard them as overgrown calculators. Computer Science was treated as an adjunct to Mathematics. Numerical analysis was considered the very heart of advanced programming.

This state of affairs no longer exists, although we still see some vestiges of it. Members of university science departments have been known to complain about people using the computer to format papers and theses. 'It was not bought to do that,' they objected. 'Its job is to do our number-crunching.'

Now that more enlightened counsels prevail, there is a need for an examination of the problems presented by text processing. My hope is that the present volume will prove useful not only to students of Computer Science but also to programmers who are working on applications in this area. Since even modern programming languages too often give only minimal support to those handling characters, the necessary techniques should be more widely disseminated.

These chapters grew out of some lectures given to Computer Science students both on text processing in general and on the SNOBOL4 language. I am grateful to my students for their patience and for their skill in debugging my program examples.

I must also record my indebtedness to Bryan Niblett, whose helpful advice and encouragement have borne me up through the weary days when I wondered whether the text would ever be processed. I am also very grateful to the Computer Centre of University College London for their cooperation in the production of this book.

1
Introduction

1.1   Terminology

This book describes the storage and processing of textual material by means of a digital computer. The basic terms used in describing text processing are often words used in common speech with a somewhat different meaning. These terms must be clarified at the outset, lest the author and his readers be similar to British and Americans, who have been described as 'a people divided by a common language'.

Text may be described as 'information coded as characters or sequences of characters'. 'Text' in this book is not used in the sense of literary material as originally written by an author ('This version differs from the true text'), nor to refer to a verse from the Bible ('My text naturally falls into three parts'). The word is here used to describe information coded in a special way, the basic unit of text being the character.

Text may therefore be contrasted with numbers, for which the basic unit is the numeric digit. Decimal numbers are coded using the decimal digits 0, 1, 2, 3, 4, 5, 6, 7, 8 and 9 (perhaps with the help of +, - and the decimal point). Text is built up from a much larger set of units, of which those used to represent decimal numbers form a subset. The characters of computer text comprise not only

- the capital (or upper case) letters   A - Z

        but also (very often)

- the lower-case letters   a - z

and include
- the decimal digits   0 - 9

    together with a motley group
- the special characters   + - ( ) / . , etc

    and a character which must not be overlooked
- the space.

The characters which make up text are thus very similar to the characters which may be produced on a typewriter. The total inventory of characters available on a particular computer is known as the <u>character set</u>. Different computers vary in their character sets. Some do not include the lower case letters, and others have a larger number of special characters.

Sequences of characters are known as <u>character strings</u>. Any English word in printed form is a character string. So is a sentence, or a paragraph, or a book. A typed number is yet another example, using as it does a subset of the full character set. But character strings are not limited to examples of these types. Any sequence of any characters is a character string. Such a string is not limited in length (although in practice there will always be a maximum, even if it is huge). The minimum length for a character string is zero - no characters at all.

Taken together, characters and character strings comprise <u>text</u>, a form of information which is of vital importance, yet not without its problems.

1.2   The uniqueness of text

The definition of 'text' in the last section is a very wide one. All that you have ever read or written was text. No form for representing information is as general and universal as text. As human beings find information in this form so commonplace it seems as surprising to call it by the special name of 'text' as it was for Molière's character M. Jourdain to discover that he always spoke prose.

However, within a computer, information may be coded in various different ways. We need the term 'text' to distinguish this type of information from binary integer numbers, floating point numbers, booleans etc. Even in such company, text is unique. Computer input typed on a keyboard device (a terminal) is in the

2

form of text, even if it will be converted to another form when inside the computer. Output for human inspection must be in the form of text when it is printed or displayed. So, for instance, binary numbers must be converted to character strings using the decimal digits, plus, minus, decimal points and spaces. Boolean values are usually represented as the strings TRUE and FALSE.

In computer terms, text may be considered to be the most basic form of information. All other types of information may be coded as text, and indeed are usually coded as such for input and output.

Because of this, almost all programs run on a computer need to process text. Compilers and interpreters need to read program statements as character strings. They also need to store lists of keywords for the programming language (such as **begin, end, real, integer**), and lists of the identifiers used in the program (names of variables, procedures etc) all of which are character strings.

Operating systems need to read and process statements in job control language. These statements will include keywords and the names both of programs available and of files to be used, all of which are represented in terms of character strings.

A user program which has been compiled and is ready to run must include routines which can handle text. These routines will for instance convert numbers from character string form to binary on input and vice versa on output. Though the user does not need to write these routines, they are nevertheless needed and are usually linked in with the user's program before execution.

Some programs handle no other information except text. An example is an editing program, allowing one to make changes to a file of text. Another example is a word-processing program, which automates typewriting and editing. In this case, text must be read in, divided into its constituent words, which are then arranged on successive lines of the display. When the characters, words, lines, paragraphs and pages have been edited to the user's satisfaction, the result may be output to a printer.

Not only is text the most basic form of computer information. It is also the most standard. Information from a computer may be written out in binary form, without being translated into character strings. However, binary output is usually specific to a particular model or series of computer. Text, on the other hand, is far more compatible. Text output in machine-readable form (on tapes, discs etc) may be transferred to another computer comparatively easily, provided of course that both sites have the hardware for handling that form of data and that the characters used are all in the character sets of both computers.

1.3 The problems of text

Though text is so fundamental when using a digital computer, processing text by computer is not necessarily straightforward. The hardware often gives the impression that it has been designed with the processing of numbers firmly in view. Handling characters may appear to be an afterthought of the designers, something which is possible but hardly easy.

This preoccupation with numbers is even apparent in the terms used. The term word has been commandeered to refer to a piece of computer store suitable for holding a number. Normally integer or floating point binary numbers are stored in these locations rather than the words of a language. A computer word is much bigger than the space necessary for storing a single character. With a computer whose store is exclusively based on words, one must decide whether to pack several characters per word (wasting processor time accessing each character) or to store only one character per word (wasting space).

If characters cause problems, character strings cause far more. A string may be any length from zero up to an arbitrary maximum. Should a program manipulating strings reserve the maximum space for every string beforehand? Or can a string dynamically acquire the space it needs as execution progresses? The former strategy causes wanton wastage of space and may at the same time impose unacceptable restrictions on the maximum length of strings. The latter method must allow some way to retrieve storage space which is no longer required. Character string processing therefore requires solutions to the problems of dynamic space allocation and retrieval.

Not only does storage lead to problems; processing causes still more. Computers provide the basic operations for processing numbers (addition, subtraction, multiplication, division, comparison etc). The hardware provides machine instructions for doing these things. The operations required for text are less familiar, and are usually not supported by means of hardware operations. Moreover, the operations may be complicated still further by the

4

form which the character string has to take in the store. That is to say, the method of space allocation which has been chosen will impose a certain structure on the character strings. The fact that the strings are held in this way may make certain operations somewhat awkward to perform.

General-purpose programming languages usually provide only minimal help for text processing. Individual characters can be handled, but strings of characters are rarely stored and operated on adequately. In this book Pascal and Fortran 77 will be used as examples of general-purpose languages. The reader is not expected to be conversant with these languages beforehand. The features will be explained as they are introduced. The aim is not to teach these two languages in any fulness, but simply to show enough to make it clear what provision they make for text processing.

Some computer languages have been developed with text handling specifically in mind. These enable text to be processed powerfully with comparative ease. An example is the SNOBOL4 language, which will be introduced in later chapters. Such a language provides string handling capabilities by means of routines which are supplied to run alongside the user's program. Earlier chapters in the book seek to explain the problems which such routines have to face, together with possible solutions to those problems.

It should be noted that the term 'text processing' is sometimes loosely used instead of 'word processing' to refer to the editing and formatting of natural language into a printable document. This is a separate (though related) subject, and is not covered in this book.

1.4   Exercises

(1)   Find out what forms of data are recognised and specifically processed by the computer to which you have access. These should be forms for which there exist corresponding hardware instructions. Make a list for each form of the hardware operations provided.

(2)   Give examples of programs

(a)   whose primary input and primary output are both text;

(b)   whose primary input (but not its primary output) is text;

(c)   whose primary output (but not its primary input) is text;

(d)   for which neither the primary input nor the primary output is text.

Note that 'primary input' is taken to exclude such things as control information, and 'primary output' is meant to exclude such things as messages and diagnostics.

2
Characters

2.1   Bytes and words

A character external to a computer may be represented by a character printed on a piece of paper, a column of a punched card, a stripe across a paper tape, a character displayed on a terminal etc.

Inside a computer, a character is represented by a short sequence of bits (0s and 1s), often 8 bits being used. The amount of space used within a computer to store a single character is commonly called a byte.

As mentioned in Chapter 1, computers have a unit of storage called the word. This is (almost always) the unit used for storing an integer or a single precision real number. The hardware instruction set of the computer will contain instructions for manipulating such words. Normally, at least one register will be large enough to hold one word. Certain hardware instructions will load a word from the store into a register, or store a register value into a word of the store.

The size of the word (called the word length) varies from computer to computer. It may be as large as 60 bits (or more). It may be as small as 16 bits (or less). However, within one computer the word length is constant.

Similarly, the byte size varies from computer to computer (6, 7 or 8 bits being the sizes in common use), but again within one computer the byte size is constant. Several bytes are usually accommodated within one word.

All computers have some way of addressing locations within the store. However, there is a major difference in that some computers have a different address for every byte and others only have a different address for every word. The former are said to have byte addressing and the latter to have only word addressing. Sometimes the former is described as a byte machine and the latter a word machine.

The following diagram shows part of the store of a computer with byte addressing. It is supposed that the computer has four bytes to every word. Each word is shown on a separate line, and each byte is represented as a box.

56	57	58	59
60	61	62	63
64	65	66	67

If the computer has word addressing with four bytes to every word, then the situation may be represented as follows.

56			
57			
58			
59			

Note that the computer with byte addressing may still address words. In the first diagram here, the addresses of the three words shown are 56, 60 and 64. How is it to be understood whether 56 is the address of a byte or of a word? The answer is, by the context. If the address is being used in a machine instruction manipulating words, then the address is that of a word. If the machine instruction operates on a byte, then the address is that of a byte.

This distinction between word and byte addressing is perhaps not quite as clear-cut as this. Knuth, in inventing his MIX machine (Knuth, 1968), gives it one address per word, but also allows a machine instruction to have a field within which the range of bytes within the word may be specified. This means that a machine instruction may indicate not only a word address, but also one or more bytes within that word on which the operation is to be performed. Although apparently a word addressing machine, MIX (and any other machine like it) is nevertheless capable of byte addressing.

2.2   Packing
Characters may be held within words in two main ways. If every word holds as many characters as possible, the characters are said to be packed. If every word holds only one character, the characters are said to be unpacked. Of course, a word cannot hold just one character and nothing else unless the word is the same size as the byte. Words containing unpacked characters may conveniently hold the character in the low-order bits, with the rest of the word filled with zero bits.

Packed	T	h	i	s
characters		i	s	
	t	e	x	t

	T
	h
	i
	s
	i
	s

Unpacked characters

. . .

Obviously, space is used more efficiently if the characters are packed. However, if the computer in question has only word addressing, access to a particular character in a packed piece of text may take a number of machine instructions, and therefore consideration of execution time may swing the decision towards holding the characters in unpacked form.

Let us consider how a computer with word addressing would retrieve a single character from a packed word. We will suppose that the word is packed with four characters as follows:

T	h	i	s

and that we are to select the second character ('h'). First we need a masking word which contains 0 bits everywhere except for the second byte. This may be represented as

0000000	1111111	0000000	0000000

Note that this is intended to represent a word containing some bytes with only '0' bits, and one byte with only '1' bits. If we perform a bitwise 'and' between these two words, we will be left with a word containing only the second character. This operation takes corresponding bits from the two words and produces a '1' result only if both bits are '1'.

0000000	h	0000000	0000000

Apart from the byte containing the 'h' character, all bytes are filled with zero bits. The contents of the word may be shifted right the requisite number of places so that the required character is in the low-order byte:

0000000	0000000	0000000	h

This is now the unpacked character 'h'.

Repeating this operation (using different masks and shifts) for all the characters in the word produces the unpacked characters corresponding to the whole packed word.

A similar sequence of operations is required to take unpacked characters and pack them into a word (see exercise 1, section 2.8).

2.3   Byte sizes

The space occupied by a single packed character, ie the byte size, varies between computers. The most common byte sizes are six bits (usually on word-addressing machines) or eight bits (usually on byte-addressing machines). There are also machines on which five 7-bit characters are packed into one 36-bit word.

If six bits are available for a character, no more than 64 different characters may be directly represented. This is enough for the ten numeric digits 0 - 9, the 26 alphabetic characters A - Z and 28 others (including such special characters as + - * / ( ) , .

and space). It is not enough to permit the representation of the lower case letters a – z in addition to the upper case letters A – Z.

If seven bits are available for the character, it is possible to represent up to 128 different characters directly. With eight bits, up to 256 characters are possible. In both these cases it is easy to have a character set at least as full as that on a normal typewriter.

2.4 Representations

We normally think of a character as a certain printed shape, such as A or *. In computer terms, this is the representation of the character as it appears externally, ie outside the computer. This <u>external representation</u> of the character is often called the character's <u>graphic</u>.

The <u>internal representation</u> of the character is the appropriate pattern of bits occupying one byte of store. We might ask, which is the character fundamentally, its graphic or its internal representation?

This is not merely an idle philosophical point. Internal representations and graphics are not in one-to-one correspondence. One internal representation may give rise to different graphics if it is output to different printing devices. This is often the case in a large computer installation, where a variety of printers of different types and from various manufacturers have been connected to one computer system. Frequently some of the less common special characters will produce a multiplicity of graphics on different printers. It is also possible for an internal representation not to correspond to any graphic at all, as we shall see later in this chapter.

The latter point alone would be sufficient for us to decide that the internal representation is more fundamental than the graphic. If a character may exist without a graphic, the internal representation must give it existence. Moreover, a computer can only operate on the internal representation of a character, irrespective of its graphic. For this reason also, the internal representation must be considered to define the character. However, in normal language we refer to characters by their graphics, and in this book we will continue to do so. A definition of a character set comprises a mapping between internal representations and graphics, but it must be borne in mind that the latter are the graphics one would expect to see, and that often practical problems arise in actually achieving them.

2.5   Characters as numbers

One byte of information may be regarded as a binary integer number. This means that a character held in a 6-bit byte may be considered to be an integer in the range 0 - 63. Similarly, an 8-bit byte containing a character could be considered to contain an integer in the range 0 - 255.

This gives a method for ordering the characters within a character set. The collating sequence for a character set is the sequence of characters arranged in ascending order of equivalent integer values. The character with equivalent value 0 will then always be the first character in the collating sequence.

The originators of both Pascal and Fortran 77 have sought to give programmers certain minimum facts which may safely be assumed to apply to all character sets. These minimum universal assumptions for the two languages are not identical, however. Both Pascal and Fortran 77 agree on the first three:

1.   The set of capital letters A - Z are in alphabetical order within the collating sequence;

2.   The numeric digits 0 - 9 are in ascending numerical order within the collating sequence;

3.   There is a blank character.

To these, Pascal adds a fourth assumption:

4.   The numeric digits 0 - 9 are contiguous within the collating sequence (ie the next character after 0 is 1, etc).

Fortran 77 would add to the first three assumptions the following:

5.   The numeric digits 0 - 9 do not fall within the capital letters A - Z (ie 9 < A or Z < 0);

6.   Blank precedes A in the collating sequence;

7.   Blank precedes 0 in the collating sequence.

In practice, all of the above seven assumptions may be relied upon as valid generalisations concerning character sets. There have been computer character sets which have transgressed some of these rules, but by now the machines concerned are so rare that the reader may be expected not to encounter them.

It may come as a surprise to discover that the ordering of the lower case letters a - z is not mentioned in the rules. The reason is, of course, that one cannot even rely on these characters being present in all character sets. If they are available, then alphabetic ordering may be presumed to exist among them.

2.6   A typical character set

Table 1 shows an actual character set which is currently used by some somputers. This approximates to the ISO-7-UK 7-bit data code defined by the British Standards Institute in their document BSI (1974). This standard is a variant of the international standard ISO 7-bit code, and is one of the family of codes loosely referred to as 'ASCII'.

Table 1 shows the character set in three columns headed 'Dec' (for 'Decimal'), 'Hex' (for 'Hexadecimal') and 'Char' (for 'Character'). The first two columns give the corresponding integer equivalent of each character in decimal and hexadecimal respectively. The column headed 'Char' needs some explanation. Where a single character appears in this column (eg A or =) this is the graphic. The blank character gives rise to special problems, because when it is 'printed' it cannot be seen. For this reason, it is represented in Table 1 by SP (decimal value 32).

The first quarter of the table (hexadecimal values 00 - 1F) and the last character (hexadecimal 7F) are represented by two or three letters or digits. These characters have special functions of various kinds, such as the following.

(a)   Transmission control characters are used in tele-communications. When text is sent down a line to a distant piece of machinery, some characters are used for special purposes. For example, STX (Start of text - hexadecimal 02) is used to signal that a string of text follows.

(b)   Layout characters cause certain peripherals (such as a teletypewriter) to change the place at which printing takes place. For example, BS (Backspace - hexadecimal 08) causes the print head to move back over the last character typed, CR (Carriage return - hexadecimal 0D) sends the print head back to the start of the line, LF (Line feed - hexadecimal 0A) moves the print head down

Dec	Hex	Char	Dec	Hex	Char	Dec	Hex	Char	Dec	Hex	Char
0	00	NUL	32	20	SP	64	40	@	96	60	`
1	01	SOH	33	21	!	65	41	A	97	61	a
2	02	STX	34	22	"	66	42	B	98	62	b
3	03	ETX	35	23	#	67	43	C	99	63	c
4	04	EOT	36	24	$	68	44	D	100	64	d
5	05	ENQ	37	25	%	69	45	E	101	65	e
6	06	ACK	38	26	&	70	46	F	102	66	f
7	07	BEL	39	27	'	71	47	G	103	67	g
8	08	BS	40	28	(	72	48	H	104	68	h
9	09	HT	41	29	)	73	49	I	105	69	i
10	0A	LF	42	2A	*	74	4A	J	106	6A	j
11	0B	VT	43	2B	+	75	4B	K	107	6B	k
12	0C	FF	44	2C	,	76	4C	L	108	6C	l
13	0D	CR	45	2D	-	77	4D	M	109	6D	m
14	0E	SO	46	2E	.	78	4E	N	110	6E	n
15	0F	SI	47	2F	/	79	4F	O	111	6F	o
16	10	DLE	48	30	0	80	50	P	112	70	p
17	11	DC1	49	31	1	81	51	Q	113	71	q
18	12	DC2	50	32	2	82	52	R	114	72	r
19	13	DC3	51	33	3	83	53	S	115	73	s
20	14	DC4	52	34	4	84	54	T	116	74	t
21	15	NAK	53	35	5	85	55	U	117	75	u
22	16	SYN	54	36	6	86	56	V	118	76	v
23	17	ETB	55	37	7	87	57	W	119	77	w
24	18	CAN	56	38	8	88	58	X	120	78	x
25	19	EM	57	39	9	89	59	Y	121	79	y
26	1A	SUB	58	3A	:	90	5A	Z	122	7A	z
27	1B	ESC	59	3B	;	91	5B	[	123	7B	{
28	1C	FS	60	3C	<	92	5C	\	124	7C		
29	1D	GS	61	3D	=	93	5D	]	125	7D	}
30	1E	RS	62	3E	>	94	5E	^	126	7E	~
31	1F	US	63	3F	?	95	5F	_	127	7F	DEL

TABLE 1. An approximation to ISO-7-UK data code.

Dec	Hex	Char	Dec	Hex	Char	Dec	Hex	Char	Dec	Hex	Char
0	00		32	20		64	40	SP	96	60	–
1	01		33	21		65	41		97	61	/
2	02		34	22		66	42		98	62	
3	03		35	23		67	43		99	63	
4	04	PF	36	24	BYP	68	44		100	64	
5	05	HT	37	25	LF	69	45		101	65	
6	06	LC	38	26	EOB	70	46		102	66	
7	07	DEL	39	27	PRE	71	47		103	67	
8	08		40	28		72	48		104	68	
9	09		41	29		73	49		105	69	
10	0A		42	2A	SM	74	4A	¢	106	6A	
11	0B		43	2B		75	4B	.	107	6B	,
12	0C		44	2C		76	4C	<	108	6C	%
13	0D		45	2D		77	4D	(	109	6D	_
14	0E		46	2E		78	4E	+	110	6E	>
15	0F	CU1	47	2F	CU3	79	4F	|	111	6F	?
16	10		48	30		80	50	&	112	70	
17	11		49	31		81	51		113	71	
18	12		50	32		82	52		114	72	
19	13		51	33		83	53		115	73	
20	14	RES	52	34	PN	84	54		116	74	
21	15	NL	53	35	RS	85	55		117	75	
22	16	BS	54	36	UC	86	56		118	76	
23	17	IL	55	37	EOT	87	57		119	77	
24	18		56	38		88	58		120	78	
25	19		57	39		89	59		121	79	
26	1A	CC	58	3A		90	5A	!	122	7A	:
27	1B		59	3B		91	5B	$	123	7B	#
28	1C		60	3C		92	5C	*	124	7C	@
29	1D		61	3D		93	5D	)	125	7D	'
30	1E		62	3E		94	5E	;	126	7E	=
31	1F	CU2	63	3F		95	5F	¬	127	7F	"

TABLE 2. EBCDIC code.

Dec	Hex	Char	Dec	Hex	Char	Dec	Hex	Char	Dec	Hex	Char
128	80		160	A0		192	C0		224	E0	
129	81	a	161	A1		193	C1	A	225	E1	
130	82	b	162	A2	s	194	C2	B	226	E2	S
131	83	c	163	A3	t	195	C3	C	227	E3	T
132	84	d	164	A4	u	196	C4	D	228	E4	U
133	85	e	165	A5	v	197	C5	E	229	E5	V
134	86	f	166	A6	w	198	C6	F	230	E6	W
135	87	g	167	A7	x	199	C7	G	231	E7	X
136	88	h	168	A8	y	200	C8	H	232	E8	Y
137	89	i	169	A9	z	201	C9	I	233	E9	Z
138	8A		170	AA		202	CA		234	EA	
139	8B		171	AB		203	CB		235	EB	
140	8C		172	AC		204	CC		236	EC	
141	8D		173	AD		205	CD		237	ED	
142	8E		174	AE		206	CE		238	EE	
143	8F		175	AF		207	CF		239	EF	
144	90		176	B0		208	D0		240	F0	0
145	91	j	177	B1		209	D1	J	241	F1	1
146	92	k	178	B2		210	D2	K	242	F2	2
147	93	l	179	B3		211	D3	L	243	F3	3
148	94	m	180	B4		212	D4	M	244	F4	4
149	95	n	181	B5		213	D5	N	245	F5	5
150	96	o	182	B6		214	D6	O	246	F6	6
151	97	p	183	B7		215	D7	P	247	F7	7
152	98	q	184	B8		216	D8	Q	248	F8	8
153	99	r	185	B9		217	D9	R	249	F9	9
154	9A		186	BA		218	DA		250	FA	
155	9B		187	BB		219	DB		251	FB	
156	9C		188	BC		220	DC		252	FC	
157	9D		189	BD		221	DD		253	FD	
158	9E		190	BE		222	DE		254	FE	
159	9F		191	BF		223	DF		255	FF	

TABLE 2 (continued).

one line.

(c)   The DEL character (Delete - hexadecimal 7F) arises from the needs of punched paper tape. Since all seven bits of DEL are set to 1, on paper tape this is represented as a stripe with all seven holes punched, which is useful for overpunching to delete an erroneous character.

Although the character set in Table 1 uses only seven bits, it can easily be used on machines with 8-bit bytes. This is usually performed by having the high-order bit set to 0.

2.7   An alternative character set

Table 2 shows another actual character set which is used by IBM computers (among others). This is the EBCDIC code (Extended Binary Coded Decimal Interchange Code), often pronounced ebb-see-dick. It is worth comparing EBCDIC with ASCII to see the ways in which such character sets may differ.

The EBCDIC character set has 256 characters, and so is twice as big as ASCII, which has 128. EBCDIC, like ASCII, includes special function characters. In Table 2 these are the characters with hexadecimal values 00 - 3F.

Many places in Table 2 have neither function nor graphic printed. This simply means that the character is not used with a special function, and there is no common graphic for it. This does not prevent such characters from being manipulated inside the computer, but input and output might cause problems.

In EBCDIC the alphabet is not contiguous in either upper or lower case. There are gaps between I and J (i and j) and between R and S (r and s). This contrasts with ASCII, in which both alphabets are contiguous throughout.

In Table 1 the basic order is

> special function characters
> blank
> special characters
> numeric digits
> special characters
> capitals
> special characters
> lower case letters
> special characters

18

In Table 2, on the other hand, the order is

> special function characters
> blank
> special characters
> lower case letters
> capital letters
> numeric digits.

In both ASCII and EBCDIC the blank character is lower in the collating sequence than all other characters with graphics.

2.8 Exercises

(1) Work out the sequence of operations needed on a computer with only word addressing to take unpacked characters and pack them into a word.

(2) Find out whether your local computer has word or byte addressing, and how many bits are used for each character. Investigate its character set and compare this with Tables 1 and 2.

(3) Try sending the full set of characters with graphics to various peripherals (the lineprinter, different types of terminal etc). Are any characters represented differently on different devices?

3

Character operations

3.1 Basic operations

If computer programs are to be able to handle single characters, computer languages must allow certain basic operations to be performed on those characters. In the case of numeric data, the essential operations are those of arithmetic (addition, subtraction, multiplication and division). When these basic arithmetic operations are provided, all other numerical operations (such as exponentiation, square roots etc) can be programmed using the basics. One could argue that not all four arithmetic operations are basic, since one could perform multiplication by repeated additions and division by repeated subtractions. Although this is true, considerations of ease of use and efficiency require us to keep the list as it is. With character operations the same applies. Some operations which are not strictly basic need to be provided as if they were.

Note that the important matter here is the provision of the operations. The grammatical form by which such an operation is invoked is of comparatively minor importance. It does not matter very much whether one must use an operator such as

    a + b

or whether one must use a function or procedure reference such as

    add(a, b)

The essential matter is that the operation be possible.

3.2　Assignment

It must be possible for the program to store a single character at a particular location in the machine's store, and to change the character stored there when required. This means that the programming language must allow variables which may have a single character as their value. An assignment statement must be available which takes a character value and stores it in the variable.

The character value which is assigned may be one which is stored in a character variable. The programming language should also permit such a value to be a character constant, in which case the character value will probably be written as a literal, ie the character itself is written directly in the programming statement without the need for an identifier (or name).

The value assigned may alternatively be from any other source which produces a character value, eg a function or operation yielding a character result.

In this way assignment for characters is analogous to assignment for numeric values. The following examples from an imaginary language (in which ':=' is used to indicate assignment) serve to show the parallels.

Numeric	Character
a := b	c := d
a := 3.14159	c := '+'
a := sqrt(b)	c := charval(i)

The various ways of referring to a character value (variable, constant, function reference etc) may be considered as examples of a character expression. This term is useful as a short means of referring to different types of character values, but in practice the rich variety displayed by numeric expressions rarely finds a counterpart in the limited forms assumed by character expressions.

3.3　Comparison

It must be possible to compare character values and to cause a change to the program's action depending on the result of that comparison.

The two values which are being compared may be characters held in variables, character constants or indeed any form which yields a character result, ie they may be character expressions.

The comparisons to be performed between two character values should obviously include tests for equality or inequality. The following tests, for instance, may well be needed:

'If the value in variable c is equal to the character '+' then...'

'If the value in variable d is not the same as the character 'P' then...'

Does it make sense to ask whether one character value is less than another? Or greater than another? Of course it can make sense if the designer of the programming language decrees the meaning which it is to carry. But will the users of that language need such a comparison?

In terms of the capital letters it would be useful to consider that one letter is 'less than' another if the former letter precedes the latter one alphabetically, so that for example B is 'less than' X and J is 'greater than' I. This is, of course, the result which we achieve if the comparison is based on the equivalent integer values of the characters, showing their order within the collating sequence.

The meaning of 'less than' or 'greater than' where characters are concerned is both of practical value and easy to implement. In some cases the computer hardware provides machine instructions which will compare characters directly in the way we require. If the hardware does not support such comparisons, the characters may easily be expanded to integer numbers which may be compared.

However, the important point for us in this chapter is not whether the operations can be performed easily, but how necessary these operations are for character manipulation. Character comparison is vitally necessary for us. It would be of most use could we be sure that all collating sequences were identical. Then a character could be identified as belonging to one half or other of the standard character set on the basis of a single comparison.

In the real world, standardisation is never as complete as we could wish. The assumptions concerning collating sequences which were listed in Chapter 2 enable us to use character comparison to perform many identification operations in a satisfactory way. For example, one can test to see whether the character held within a variable is a numeric digit by the double comparison:

'If c is greater than or equal to '0'
and c is less than or equal to '9' then...'

3.4 Reading and writing

A program which is processing characters must obviously be able to input them and output them.

Input needs to take place from the external record (a punched card, a line on paper tape or a line typed on to a keyboard for instance) to character variables in the machine's store. A read operation will take the next available character in the record and copy it into the variable.

Each record is of finite length. What happens when a character is to be read and the pointer is at the end of the record? It is essential that the program be able to detect this condition. There are two possible actions which could be taken in this situation.

(1)   One could treat the end of record as if it were itself a character. This could be, for instance, one of the special function characters from the first quadrant of Tables 1 and 2 in Chapter 2 (such as the Carriage return character, C R). The value of the variable could then be tested to see whether the end of record has been reached. One drawback to this method is the choice of special function character. If the input text contains an instance of this same character, then this will be indistinguishable from the end of a record. Even more important, it is very hard to specify in a programming language a constant form for a character which does not have a graphic.

(2)   Alternatively, a function could be provided for testing to see whether the end of record has been reached, returning a true/false result. Now there is no need to transmit special characters when the end of record is encountered. A read operation at end of record could cause the first character of the next record to be transmitted. This means that if the function is not examined, successive characters are read as if they were on the same long record.

The end of file causes problems similar to those caused by the end of record. What happens when the last character of the last record has been read and a read instruction demands yet another character? Obviously a diagnostic message must be issued, but the program needs to be able to test for the end of file condition to avoid causing an error. As for the end of record, this can be done by using another special function character to represent the end of file or by providing another function which will respond with a true/false result.

An output operation will take character values and append them to a record being sent to an output device (such as the lineprinter or to be displayed on a terminal). Some mechanism needs to be provided to terminate the record, causing the old record to be written out and permitting a new record to be started. A similar mechanism may be needed to terminate the whole file of records. Procedures can be supplied to perform these operations.

3.5   Type conversion

Computer languages usually provide transfer (or type conversion) functions to convert data from one type to another, eg from integer to floating point and vice versa. For character manipulation, two such transfer functions are needed. These are to convert a character into its corrresponding integer, and to convert an integer into the corresponding character. (The integer corrresponding to a character is of course its index within the collating sequence.)

It is possible to perform these transfer operations using the previously defined operations of assignment and comparison. To convert from a character to an integer the following method may be used.

An array of character variables is used, containing the full character set in collating sequence order. The character value to be converted to integer is then compared with each of the array values in turn until a match for equality is found. The index within the array is then the integer corresponding to the character.

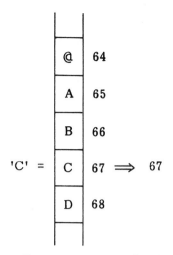

'C' =   @ 64
         A 65
         B 66
         C 67 ⟹ 67
         D 68

The reverse operation is then performed by using the integer as an index within the array. The character retrieved then corresponds to the integer value.

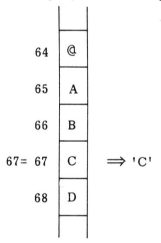

64 @
65 A
66 B
67= 67 C ⟹ 'C'
68 D

Although type conversion between characters and integers can be performed by more basic operations, it is nevertheless important that such functions be in our minimal list, to be provided by the programming language. It will be necessary to use such operations frequently, and in such a case the user should not have to write the code himself. Moreover, code written by the user will be much less efficient than a facility provided for him.

Converting a character to an integer by the method above requires many comparisons. If the character set comprises 128 characters, then on average 64 comparisons will be needed before a match is found. On the other hand, the bits which constitute the character may be expanded with high-order zero bits, forming the integer equivalent in one operation.

Converting an integer into a character by means of the table look-up method shown above is not so inefficient in time, but like the method for the reverse operation, it requires an array of characters, which is a waste of space. Selecting the low-order bits of the integer value produces the character value directly.

The need for these two operations has still to be vindicated. Once one has transformed a character into an integer, it can readily be understood that one may need to change it back into a character again. Why would one want to transform it into an integer in the first place?

A character needs to be converted to an integer if it is to be used as an index for table look-up. This is similar to the method used earlier for converting an integer back to a character, but applications generally use other kinds of arrays.

For instance, let us suppose it necessary to transform text so that lower case letters are changed into the corresponding capital letters. In this case we need an array of characters in collating sequence order, except that the lower case characters must be replaced by the upper case alphabet. Each character in the input text must be changed to an integer which will then be used as an index to select from the array the character to be output. All characters will then map into themselves with the exception of the lower case letters, which will be mapped into the corresponding capitals.

As another example, let us consider that we want to classify characters into various types. We will call numeric digits type 1, alphabetic characters (upper or lower case) type 2, a blank type 3, punctuation marks type 4 and all other characters type 5. In this case we need an array of integers initialised so that in the place corresponding to each character we have the integer value indicating that character's type. Any character may rapidly be classified by converting it to an integer and using this as the index to select an integer flag from the array.

3.6 Exercises

For these exercises you may assume the following:

c	a character variable
i	an integer variable
read(c)	places the next input character in c
write(c)	adds c on to the end of the output line
ord(c)	a function giving the integer value of c
chr(i)	a function giving the character equivalent of i
v:=x	form of the assignment statement
if...then...	form of a test

(1)   A program is to be written to take text in capitals and output it in coded form. To do this, the letters will be rotated one place so that A will be printed as B, B as C, C as D etc and Z as A. Write instructions to take a character which has been read into c and transform it so that it is suitable for output. Remember that all characters except for the capital letters are to be left unchanged. (Assume the letters to be contiguous.)

(2)   Write instructions to read numeric digits terminated by a blank and construct them as an integer number in i.

(3)   A hexadecimal number is one which uses the base 16. It employs the decimal digits 0 - 9 and also the letters A - F to represent the digits 10 - 15. Write instructions to read hexadecimal digits terminated by a blank and to construct them as an integer number in the variable i.

4
Characters in programming languages

4.1 Programming languages

Recently developed programming languages include some facilities for text processing, although in general-purpose languages the apparatus provided tends to be somewhat primitive and oriented towards handling single characters rather than character strings. However, even this state of affairs has an advantage for the student, since more sophisticated facilities have to be developed in full view of the programmer (and probably by means of his own efforts) and therefore the problems and techniques involved are more open to study.

By way of illustration in this book, two general-purpose languages have been selected. These are Fortran 77 and Pascal. Enough information will be given about these languages as examples are introduced so that readers who are unfamiliar with them may nevertheless follow the program portions.

Later in the book, SNOBOL4 will be introduced. This is a language specially designed to facilitate the manipulation of character strings. Though text processing is very much easier in SNOBOL, more can be learnt about the methods of text processing by limiting oneself to a less obliging language initially.

This chapter will examine the way Fortran 77 and Pascal provide the character operations which in Chapter 3 were claimed to be essential.

4.2 Fortran 77

Fortran 77 is defined in ANSI (1978), but users will find it preferable to use an introductory textbook such as Balfour and Marwick (1979).

Fortran 77 grew out of an earlier language now known as Fortran 66, often loosely referred to as Fortran IV. The earlier language did not allow a character type for variables. Characters could be placed in variables of any type (integer, real, double precision, complex or logical), but if you then managed to process them it was thanks to your ingenuity rather than to any help which the language afforded. In fact character handling in Fortran 66 has been compared to shelling peas whilst wearing boxing gloves.

Fortran 77 introduced a new type of data: CHARACTER. Character variables which may hold a single character may be declared by means of the CHARACTER declaration, eg

CHARACTER C, CH, X

Character constants are written by placing the character between apostrophes, eg 'A', 'y', '+', ' ' (a blank). The apostrophe character itself is represented by two apostrophes (between apostrophes), ie ''''.

4.2.1 Assignment

Assignment is permitted to a character variable from a character expression. Examples of character expressions are a character variable, a character constant, or a reference to a function which delivers a character result. For example:

```
C = 'B'
CH = C
X = 'x'
CH = CHAR(I)
```

4.2.2 Comparison

Character values may be compared in Fortran 77 using the IF statement. Relational operators used in this statement are:

.EQ.	equal to
.NE.	not equal to
.LT.	less than
.GT.	greater than
.LE.	less than or equal to
.GE.	greater than or equal to

Typical comparisons are

```
IF (CH .EQ. 'B') COUNT = 5
IF (X .NE. CHAR(I)) X = '+'
IF (C .GE. '0') I = I + 1
```

Comparisons are made on the basis of the collating sequence of the characters. Combinations of tests may be made by means of the operators .OR. and .AND. eg

```
IF (C .EQ. '+' .OR. C .EQ. '-') SIGN = SIGN + 3
IF (CH .LE. '9' .AND. CH .GE. '0') NUM = 1
```

In addition, Fortran 77 provides four functions which will compare two characters (or character strings) using the ASCII collating sequence, irrespective of whether the computer internal representation uses the ASCII code. The functions return a logical result, .TRUE. or .FALSE. The functions are:

LLT (C1, C2)	C1 is less than C2
LGT (C1, C2)	C1 is greater than C2
LLE (C1, C2)	C1 is less than or equal to C2
LGE (C1, C2)	C1 is greater than or equal to C2

Functions LEQ or LNE are not required, of course, as .EQ. and .NE. may be used instead, since equality or inequality are the same no matter what collating sequence is used.

As an example, let us test whether the character in CH is a capital letter or not. The capitals are contiguous in the ASCII character set but not in EBCDIC. So if the computer uses EBCDIC internal representation the test

```
IF (CH .GE. 'A' .AND. CH .LE. 'Z') ...
```

may go wrong. The test which will work correctly is

```
IF (LGE(CH,'A') .AND. LLE(CH,'Z')) ...
```

4.2.3 Reading and writing

In Fortran 77 a wide range of facilities is provided for input and output. The methods described here for reading and writing characters are far from being the only ones, but are the most straightforward ones. Other methods which could have been chosen do not give any greater flexibility or power.

The READ statement takes the folowing form (among others):

READ (<u>unit</u>, <u>format</u>) <u>list</u>

where <u>unit</u> is the input/output stream from which information is to be read, format is the label of a FORMAT statement describing the layout of the information and list is a list of variables to be given values. For the unit we may put *, which indicates that input is to be from the designated input unit, ie from the main input stream. If CH is a character variable we can specify this as the list in order to read a character. Any label will do, so the READ statement may then be

READ (*, 150) CH

Now we need a FORMAT with the label 150. To read a single character the FORMAT required is

150   FORMAT(A1)

There is only one problem here, but it is a major one. Each time a READ statement is started, a new record is begun. The READ statement above will read the first character of a record, but that is all. If the READ statement is obeyed a second time, it will start on a second record and read the first character of that. We are unable to read any other than the first character on each input line.

It is possible to read more than one character per record. Let us suppose that the designated input file is on punched cards. Each card has 80 characters on it. We can create an array of 80 character variables by means of the declaration

CHARACTER CARD(80)

Now we have 80 array elements, CARD(1) ... CARD(80), each able to hold a single character. The statements may be changed to

READ (*, 150) CARD
150   FORMAT(80A1)

Each time the READ is obeyed, the whole of the CARD array will be filled, and the FORMAT indicates that 80 single characters should be taken from the record. So we read all the characters on the new record each time the READ is activated.

This is all very well, but many files do not have records of a fixed length. Lines punched on paper tape or typed at a terminal, and those same lines when subsequently stored on disc, vary in length. How can we read varying length records in Fortran 77?

The answer appears to be that you can do this only if you know what length the record will be before reading it. If the record will not exceed 80 characters in length and the length of the next record is stored in an integer variable I, then the statements

```
      READ (*, 150) (CARD(J), J = 1, I)
150   FORMAT(80A1)
```

will read characters into CARD(1), CARD(2) ... CARD(I). J is an integer variable used as a counter. The READ stops when I elements of CARD have been filled, and it does not matter that part of the FORMAT is unused. It is possible to read records of varying length in this way, but there is no way provided by which a program can discover the length of the next record before reading it.

If the program tries to read a record of 80 characters when the actual record is shorter, this is presumably an error. However, many systems will pad out the input record with trailing blanks so that the READ can be satisfied. This is very kind, but the program cannot then discover which blanks formed part of the original record and which have been added.

Characters can be printed out by means of the WRITE statement, which is analogous to the READ statement, eg

```
      WRITE (*, 250) C, CH, X
250   FORMAT(' ', 3A1)
```

The * here indicates the designated output unit, ie the main output stream. In this case the three variables have their values written out on the same line. Each time a WRITE statement begins, a new output line is started. This time the FORMAT starts by specifying a blank character. This is used because the first character of every line sent to a printing device is used to control the paper movement. If each line begins with a blank, the printing will be performed single spaced.

It is possible to test for the end of file condition by supplying in the READ statement the label of a statement to which control will be passed when this condition is met.

```
      READ (*, 150, END=990) CARD
```

When the READ statement finds that there are no more records in the file, control will pass to statement 990.

A special END FILE statement is provided for writing an end of file record at the end of an output file.

4.2.4 Type conversion

Two transfer functions are provided by Fortran 77, ICHAR to take a character argument and return the equivalent integer, and CHAR to take an integer argument and return the equivalent character. Characters and integers correspond in the way one would expect from the collating sequence and from their bit patterns. Here are some examples.

```
I = ICHAR(CH) - ICHAR('0')
IF (CHAR(J) .EQ. '*') MAST = 1
C = CHAR(ICHAR(C) + 1)
```

The last statement above puts into C the character which comes after its current value in the collating sequence (so that if C contains '0', this statement will change it to '1').

4.3 Pascal

Pascal was designed by Niklaus Wirth as a simple, regular and efficiently implemented language. The international standard for Pascal is ISO/DIS 7185, of which BSI (1982) is a copy. Before this standard emerged Jensen and Wirth (1978) was often regarded informally as the standard, as well as being an introductory book. Now there are very many introductory texts, good, bad and indifferent.

Pascal has four basic data types: integer, real, Boolean and char. A variable of type char has as its value a single character. A declaration is used to specify the types of variables, eg

```
var  c, ch, x: char;
     i, j: integer;
```

Character constants are written just as in Fortran 77, eg 'A', 'y', ' ' (a blank), '''' (an apostrophe).

4.3.1 Assignment

Pascal also permits assignment to a character variable from a character expression. Examples of character expressions are a character variable, a character constant, or a reference to a function which delivers a character result. For example:

```
c := 'B';
ch := c;
x := 'x';
ch := chr(i);
```

4.3.2 Comparison

The relational operators used in Pascal are:

=	equal to
<>	not equal to
<	less than
>	greater than
<=	less than or equal to
>=	greater than or equal to

These may be used to compare character values:

```
if ch = 'B' then isign := isign + 3;
if x <> chr(i) then x := '+';
if c >= '0' then i := i + 1;
```

Comparisons are made on the basis of the collating sequence of the characters. Combinations of tests may be made by means of the operators **or** and **and** eg

```
if (c = '+') or (c = '-') then sign := sign + 3;
if (ch <= '9') and (ch >= '0') then num := 1;
```

Note the parentheses around the elemental comparisons. These are needed because of the relative priority of operators defined for Pascal.

There is provision within Pascal for the simplification of multiple comparisons. In order to test whether ch contains a punctuation character, it is not necessary to write a long test such as

```
if (ch = '.') or (ch = ',')
or (ch = ':') or (ch = ';')
or (ch = '(') or (ch = ')') then ...
```

Instead one can write

```
if ch in ['.', ',', ':', ';', '(', ')'] then ...
```

The item within square brackets is of set type. In effect, the Pascal compiler sets up a look-up table on to which the characters are mapped. If the character value in ch is in the set, then the corresponding position in the table will have a flag to indicate this.

We can test to see whether the character is a numeric digit by means of the test

if ch **in** ['0', '1', '2', '3', '4', '5', '6', '7', '8', '9'] **then** ...

Because we can be sure that the numeric digits are contiguous within the collating sequence, this can be abbreviated to

if ch **in** ['0' .. '9'] **then** ...

If one could be sure that the capital letters are contiguous one could write the test for a capital letter as

if ch **in** ['A' .. 'Z'] **then** ...

If the program may be run on a computer for which the capitals are not contiguous, then the set may need to be written out in full.

A word of caution is needed here. Pascal compilers will not handle sets above a certain size, the limit depending on the particular compiler. Using sets as we have in the statements above may require the compiler to create sets with as many members as there are characters in the collating sequence. This may be 128 or even 256, which may be more than the maximum size of a set. In Pascal terminology, the relevant question is whether or not **set of char** can be handled.

4.3.3   Reading and writing

In Pascal the next character in the input may be read into the variable ch by means of the statement

    read(ch);

Repeated use of this statement will read all the characters of the record in turn. When there are no more characters to be read from the record, a Boolean function eoln ('end of line') becomes **true**. A further read at this point will cause a blank to be read (in place of the end of line) and eoln will become **false** once more. The next read accesses the first character of the next record, and so on. When end of file is reached, a Boolean function eof becomes **true**.

At any point within a record the statement

readln;

will ignore any further characters on the record and will move to the start of a new record, leaving the first character of that record in a position to be accessed by the next read. Alternatively

readln(ch);

will read the next character from the current record and skip any subsequent characters up to but not including the start of the next record.

Output is quite similar. The statement

write(ch);

adds the character to the end of the current output line. To terminate the line one may use

writeln;

Alternatively, the statement

writeln(ch);

will append the character in ch to the end of the output line and then terminate the line.

There is no way within Pascal of writing an end of file mark, but this is not needed as operating systems will do this when a program terminates.

4.3.4 Type conversion

Pascal provides two transfer functions, ord to take a character argument and return the equivalent integer, and chr to take an integer argument and return the equivalent character. These correspond closely to ICHAR and CHAR respectively of Fortran 77. Here are some examples.

```
i := ord(ch) - ord('0');
if chr(j) = '*' then mast := 1;
c := chr(ord(c) + 1);
```

The last statement puts into c the character which comes after its current value in the collating sequence. Pascal provides a function succ for this very operation, so that the last statement may be replaced by

```
c := succ(c);
```

Similarly, the function pred returns the character preceding the current one.

4.4   Exercises

For the following exercises, if you are not familiar with Fortran 77 or Pascal, invent features (such as control structures) which have not yet been introduced.

(1)   Repeat exercise 3.6 (1) using Fortran 77.

(2)   Repeat exercise 3.6 (2) using Fortran 77.

(3)   Repeat exercise 3.6 (3) using Fortran 77.

(4)   Repeat exercise 3.6 (1) using Pascal.

(5)   Repeat exercise 3.6 (2) using Pascal.

(6)   Repeat exercise 3.6 (3) using Pascal.

5

String operations

5.1 Basic operations

With some reservations (notably Fortran 77 input) it can be said that the basic operations for single characters are adequately provided within the programming languages Fortran 77 and Pascal. However, text processing is more than the manipulation of characters one by one. We need to be able to treat character strings of indefinite length as our data. The basic operations to be performed on such character strings will be the subject for this chapter. In order to avoid tedious repetition of the phrase 'character strings' this will be shortened to 'strings'.

Given strings of unspecified length (and most general-purpose languages do not give us them) what would be the basic 'arithmetic' needed by a programmer to be able to use those strings for text processing?

5.2 Assignment

It must be possible for the program to store a string in a variable and to change the value of that variable to another string when required. In other words, an assignment statement should be provided to take a string value and store it in a variable.

The string value which is assigned may be one which is already stored in a variable. We also require the programming language to permit string constants, in which case the string value will probably be written as a literal, ie the string itself is written directly into the program statement without the need for an identifier (name). The value assigned may alternatively be from a function or any other operation which yields a string result.

It must be emphasised here that the values about which we are speaking are of indefinite length, from no characters at all to an implementation-defined limit which should at the very least be several hundred characters long. Given a variable which can accommodate a string value, it should be possible at any time to assign any string value to that variable.

The assignment required for strings is analogous to that provided for numeric values or for single characters. Assuming a suitable notation for an imaginary language, we could have the following parallels:

Numeric	Character	String
a:=3.14159	c:='+'	s:="A string"
a:=b	c:=d	s:=t
a:=sqrt(b)	c:=charval(i)	s:=substr(t,1,3)

In this chapter string constants are surrounded by double quotation marks to distinguish them from character constants, which are surrounded by apostrophes. The null string (of zero length) will be represented by "" , ie by two consecutive double quotes. The variables a and b will be assumed to be real, i and j integer, c and d character and s and t string.

As in the case of character values, we might use the term string expression to refer to different types of string values (constants, variables, functions etc).

Some machines have hardware instructions for moving whole character strings stored as contiguous characters within the store. String assignment will be faster if such instructions are used rather than copying the strings a character at a time.

5.3   Comparison

It must be possible to compare string values and to cause a change to the program's action depending on the result of that comparison.

The two values which are being compared may be strings held in variables, string constants or indeed any form which yields a string result, ie they may be string expressions.

The comparisons to be performed between two string values should obviously include tests for equality or inequality. It would be of greatest value if a comparison between unequal strings showed that the string which should precede the other in alphabetical order is the string which is 'less than' the other. How can such a test be applied to strings which may be of different length? Let us consider two strings with pointers at the head of each.

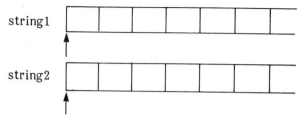

We then apply the following steps:

(1)   If the pointers are at the end of both strings, then the strings are equal;

(2)   If the pointer is at the end of string1, then string1 is less than string2;

(3)   If the pointer is at the end of string2, then string2 is less than string1;

(4)   If the character after the string1 pointer is equal to the character after the string2 pointer, then move the pointers one character position to the right and return to (1);

(5)   The result of comparing the two characters in (4) is the result of comparing the strings.

The underlying character-by-character comparison depends of course on the collating sequence for that computer. With this caveat, the method produces an alphabetic ordering which agrees with normal conventions, so that, for instance, the following are all true:

        "ADA" < "IDA"
        "JANES" < "JONES"
        "JOHN" < "JOHNS"

When comparing strings of different lengths, the effect is as if the shortest string were padded to the right with characters which precede all those in the collating sequence.

Some machines have instructions in their hardware repertoire for comparing strings of the same length on a character-by-character basis. String comparisons provided by a programming language will be most efficient if they can make use of any such hardware assistance.

5.4 Type conversion

A programming language which supports characters and character strings must provide for type conversion between a single character and a character string of length one character, and vice versa. This may seem unduly pedantic, as it may appear that characters are a subset of strings, and hence of the same type. However, a character variable may be given a fixed allocation of one byte of space, whereas a string variable needs to have some mechanism whereby the space allocated to it can change dynamically. The data structures used for storing characters and for storing strings may well be different, and hence there is a need for type conversion between them.

This conversion may be performed implicitly by the language system, but the fact remains that there is a conversion to be carried out. In this chapter the functions ctos (character to string) and stoc (string to character) will be assumed. Examples are:

s := ctos('A')
c := stoc("+")

The function ctos will always succeed, but the string argument of stoc must have a length of one character.

Type conversions between strings and numbers are also needed. A number punched on a card or typed at a terminal is basically in the form of a character string. When it is read by the computer its type is usually changed to an internal binary representation (integer or real). The reverse process takes place when a number is printed out.

These type conversion operations are performed implicitly by the input/output facilities provided with the programming language being used. Some string processing applications require such operations to be available under program control. In the past one of the ways of converting a number into a character string within a primitive language (such as Fortran 66) was to write that number out on magnetic tape or disc, rewind the device and read in the number as characters. Vast quantities of manpower have been spent on writing 'free format' input routines for such languages. Such time-consuming and circuitous methods would not have been necessary had the type conversion routines used by the run-time system been available to the programmer.

These operations will be considered here as functions called stoi (string to integer), stor (string to real), itos (integer to string) and rtos (real to string). Examples are:

```
i := stoi("7650")
s := itos(i)
a := stor("3.14159")
t := rtos(sqrt(a+b))
```

5.5   Concatenation

Concatenation is for character strings what addition is for numbers. Two strings are joined together end to end to form a single new string. So, for instance, the strings "cat" and "sup" concatenated in that order form the string "catsup".

This operation could be performed by an operator, but for the sake of similarity with other operations it will be represented here by means of a function concat.

```
s := concat("cat","sup")
s := concat(s, ctos('.'))
```

5.6   Substring selection

The need often arises to select a portion of a string, such as 'the first five characters of string s' or 'characters 15 to 21 of string t'. This is the operation of selecting a substring from a string. Obviously the substring selected is itself a string. There are three operands for this operation:

- the initial string;
- the starting position of the substring within the string;
- the end position of the substring within the string.

Alternatively, the three operands could be specified as:

- the initial string;
- the starting position of the substring within the string;
- the length of the substring.

There is not much to choose between these alternatives. In this chapter the second convention will be followed. We will postulate a function substr which may be used as follows:

t := substr("ABCDEF",3,2)

This returns the string value "CD". The statement

t := substr(s,5,1)

will result in t being assigned the fifth character of s as a character string. If the fifth character is needed as a character value (as opposed to a string value) then the function stoc must be used:

c := stoc(substr(s,5,1))

The operands for function substr may be impossible to apply. Consider for instance

substr("ABCDEF",7,2)

How can we take a substring of two characters starting at position 7 from a string which is only six characters long? Sometimes the operands can be partially satisfied, as in

substr("ABCDEF",4,10)

We can start a substring at the fourth character of the string, but it will not be ten characters long.

In such cases the function may return the longest substring which satisfies the operation. This means that the result of

substr("ABCDEF",7,2)

is the null string "" and the result of

substr("ABCDEF",4,10)

is the string "DEF" of length 3.

In order to be able to avoid trying to select a substring which is outside the string, we need a way of finding the length of a string. We will suppose this to be a function called length. Then

length("ABC")   yields the result 3 and
length("")   yields the result 0.

Then we may use statements such as

if length(s) > i+1 then t := substr(s,i,2)

5.7   Indexing

Sometimes it is necessary to find the position at which a given substring appears within a string. An example of this is to find the position at which the substring "CAT" appears in the string "INDICATE", and the answer would be 'starting at the fifth character'. This operation is called finding the index of a substring.

The operands needed are the target string and the substring. The result is an integer value which gives the character position within the target string at which the substring occurs. This operation could be provided by means of a function called index:

index("INDICATE","CAT")

would then return the value 5.

If the substring does not appear in the target string, the result of the function should not be to treat this as an error, but rather a value should be returned which can be tested by the program. The value zero is perhaps the best to indicate this condition, so that

index("search me", "clue")

would return the value 0.

The string may contain more than one instance of the substring. Should the function reference

index("multinational", "ti")

return the value 4 or 8? The answer is of course that the value returned will depend on the direction of the indexing algorithm. If we start search from the right hand end of the target string, we will find the "ti" at position 8 first. If we search from left to right, then that at position 4 will be found first. No doubt it is the influence of our Roman alphabet which makes us consider a left-to-right search as more natural. Computer machine instructions handling character strings also operate in this direction. So the function index will find the leftmost occurrence of any substring.

Strictly speaking, index is not a basic operation, since it can be programmed using the other operations of assignment, substring selection and comparison. However, it is such a commonly needed operation that it is regarded here as being basic.

5.8   Reading and writing

The records which are read or written by computer may themselves be considered character strings of varying length, from zero characters up to some system limit. It would therefore be reasonable for a read operation to take one input record and to place the characters from it into a string variable. The procedure readstr might be proposed for this:

readstr(s)

The end of record terminates the string in the input. No other string terminator is needed, nor is a test necessary for the end of record. A way is needed to test for end of file, as when reading characters.

Similarly, a string could on output produce one record. The procedure name writestr might be suggested:

writestr(s)

The only drawback to this is when one wants to print out the contents of several variables on the same line. Suppose it is necessary to have the values of i (an integer), s (a string) and b (a real) on the same output record. By using the type conversion and concatenation operations it could be ensured that the argument for writestr was still one string:

writestr (concat (itos(i), concat (s, rtos(b))))

This becomes very cumbersome. Alternatively, the procedures for reading and writing could be abnormal ones which allow arguments of any number or type and which perform the appropriate conversions of type. Then the examples in this section might be rewritten as:

read (s)
write (s)
write (i, s, b)

5.9   Exercises

For each of the following exercises use the operators proposed in this chapter, supplemented by informal devices of your own choosing for other needed language features such as control structures.

(1)   In section 5.6 it was said that the index operation is not basic, but can be programmed using the other string operations. Do this.

(2)   Write statements which will take an integer number in i and will print it out separating groups of three digits with

45

commas (from right to left). This means, for instance, that 1579862043 will print as 1,579,862,043.

(3) Write a procedure to reverse the characters of any string handed to it as an argument. This should for example turn "DOG" into "GOD".

(4) Write a function to select and return a single character at a specified position within a character string. If an error occurs, the character with value zero is to be returned.

6

Strings in programming languages

6.1 Fortran 77

The CHARACTER statement was introduced in section 4.2 as if it were simply a means whereby Fortran 77 variables holding single characters may be defined. In fact, the information presented earlier gave only a subset of the CHARACTER statement. One may define variables which will hold a character string of a predetermined length. For example, STR may be defined as a character string variable of length five by the statement

CHARACTER*5 STR

If the *5 is omitted from this statement, the default length for the character string is 1, so reducing to the earlier form by which single-character variables were defined.

String constants in Fortran 77 are also a direct extension of the character constants introduced earlier (and both are called 'character constants' in Fortran 77). Examples of string constants are

'This is a string'
'That''s right'
'0123456789'

Note that an apostrophe within a string is represented by means of two adjacent apostrophes. String constants may not have a length of zero, so that the null constant '' is not permitted.

It is not possible in this language to define string variables whose lengths vary according to what has been assigned to them. There is a mechanism which looks at first sight as if it might allow this, but closer inspection leads to disillusionment. The following declaration is permitted:

CHARACTER*(*) STR

The length of STR is here specified as (*), which means that it will vary. However, this is not permitted for ordinary variables, but is allowed if this statement occurs within a function or subroutine for which STR is a dummy argument, and so represents the string which will be passed over when the subprogram (function or subroutine) is called. If different length strings are used as the actual arguments on different calls to this subprogram, the length of STR will vary. But on any one invocation of the subprogram, STR will be fixed in length, having the same length as the actual argument.

Arrays of character variables may be declared. For example, the statement

CHARACTER NM(20)

creates an array called NM with 20 elements, each of them capable of holding a single character. Individual elements of this array may be referred to as NM(1), NM(2), NM(3) etc. This should be carefully distinguished from

CHARACTER*20 NM

which sets up a single variable able to hold a character string of length 20.

Fortran 77 uses CHARACTER to denote a type comprising both single characters and character strings. In this chapter CHARACTER will be used to mean the Fortran 77 entity, and 'character' will continue to mean a single character.

6.1.1 Assignment

Assignment to a string variable in Fortran 77 is most straightforward if the string assigned is the same length as the variable receiving it. So the statements

CHARACTER*5 STR
STR = 'ABCDE'

will put the string 'ABCDE' into STR. If the string is not the same length as the variable, then the practice followed is the same as that used by the ancient Greek inn-keeper Procrustes. If the bed was too long, he put the guest on the rack. If it was too short, he chopped their legs off. The assignment

STR = 'PULL'

causes the string of length four to be padded to the right with a blank character so that the result matches the length of STR. The string assigned is then 'PULL '. The opposite procedure is followed with

STR = 'SHORTEN LEGS'

In this case the string is truncated from the right until it will fit in STR. The string assigned is then 'SHORT'.

The CHARACTER value assigned may be a constant, a CHARACTER variable or any kind of CHARACTER expression within the limits defined by the language.

One restriction is placed on CHARACTER assignment statements. The variable to which the value is being assigned may not appear in the expression on the right of the statement.

6.1.2 Comparison

That which was said in section 4.2.2 about the comparison of single character values in Fortran 77 applies also to strings. There is, however, the extra complication of comparing strings with different lengths. Fortran 77 pads the shorter string to the right with enough blanks to ensure that both strings are the same length before comparison. The strings are then compared character by character according to the machine's collating sequence. The statement

IF ('DOG' .LT. 'DOGE') ...

has therefore the same effect as

IF ('DOG ' .LT. 'DOGE') ...

The six relational operators described in 4.2.2 apply here also. CHARACTER expressions may occur before and after them.

It is also possible to use the logical functions LLT, LGT, LLE and NNE mentioned earlier. These each take two CHARACTER expressions as arguments. The shorter argument is padded with blanks to the right. The strings are then compared character by character using the ASCII collating sequence.

6.1.3 Type conversion

In Fortran 77 there is obviously no need to convert between a string containing one character and an entity of type character, since string and character types are both subsumed under the one type CHARACTER.

Type conversion between CHARACTER and numeric value is provided for, but not by means of functions. It was said in section 5.3 that these type conversion operations are performed implicitly by the input/output routines. In Fortran normal input or output is carried out under the control of a FORMAT (as in section 4.2.3). The designers of Fortran 77 sought to provide type conversion to and from CHARACTER values by means of FORMATs. Therefore such conversion is performed by means of READ and WRITE statements. However, instead of information being transmitted to and from an external file, the file used is an internal one, namely the CHARACTER variable.

Some examples may be given here to show how the facility works.

```
      CHARACTER*7 STG
      J = -36251
      WRITE (STG, 55) J
55    FORMAT (I7)
```

Format I7 specifies an integer value within seven columns, so that the value of the integer variable J will be transformed into a character string of length seven. Instead of being written out on the standard print stream, this string value is 'written' on the internal file STG. The consequence is that STG acquires the value ' -36251'. The statements

```
      READ (STG, 60) A
60    FORMAT (F7.3)
```

will place a floating point value in the real variable A. Format specification F7.3 indicates that a floating point value is to be constructed from seven characters, of which the last three should be assumed to be after the decimal point. Normally these characters would be taken from an input record, but instead of an external stream being specified, STG is designated as an internal file. The characters ' -36251' of STG will be used to construct the binary real value -36.251 which will be placed in A.

Input/output in Fortran 77 includes an enormous range of facilities far too numerous to describe here, many of which can be used with CHARACTER internal files. This chapter simply seeks to show the kind of way in which the operations are performed rather than give the full information on the various options.

6.1.4   Concatenation

CHARACTER values may be concatenated by means of the operator //. As an example

```
CHARACTER*5 STR
CHARACTER*7 STG
STR = 'ABC' // 'DEFG'
```

will construct the character string 'ABCDEFG' of length 7 which will then be truncated to 'ABCDE' and placed in STR. The statement

```
IF (STR // '.2' .EQ. STG) ...
```

will then test whether the value in STG is equal to 'ABCDE.2'.

It is possible to concatenate CHARACTER variables whose length is declared as (*) (ie dummy arguments within a subprogram) but only if this is within an assignment statement. Such variables may not be concatenated within an IF statement, for instance.

6.1.5   Substring selection

Substrings of CHARACTER variables may be selected by giving the indices of the starting character and the end character of the substring. These are enclosed in parentheses and separated by a colon. So, for example, the following statements

```
CHARACTER*10 NM, ARTH
CHARACTER*3 SB
NM = 'ARTHRITIS.'
SB = NM(7:9)
```

will place in SB the value 'TIS', and

```
J = 4
ARTH = NM(1:J) // 'U' // NM(5:6) // 'AN'
```

will place in ARTH the value 'ARTHURIAN '. The final blank in this value is padding, as the result of the expression is nine characters long and ARTH can only accommodate a string of length ten. The first character in a string is reckoned to be at position one.

A substring may appear on the left hand side of an assignment statement:

NM(9:10) = 'C:-'

This changes the value in NM to 'ARTHRITIC:'. Since the substring of NM is of length two, the third character in the constant will not be assigned; the value will be truncated.

The restriction on assignments mentioned in 6.1.1 must now be amended to take into account substrings. The rule is that none of the single-character positions to which values are being assigned may be included in the expression on the right hand side of the assignment statement.

What if the starting point or ending point specified for the substring lies outside the string? For instance, substrings such as

NM(0:4)

or SB(2:8)

Fortran 77 decrees that this must not happen. The result is an error, and presumably the action taken depends on the implementation. It is the programmer's reponsibility to avoid such a situation happening. As an aid towards this, a function LEN is provided. This takes one argument, a CHARACTER expression, and returns an integer value giving the length of the resulting string. So, in terms of the variables defined above:

LEN(ARTH)   yields   10
LEN(SB)   3
LEN(ARTH(2:5))   4
LEN(SB // ARTH // NM(3:7)) 18

This is of particular value for dummy CHARACTER arguments whose lengths are declared as (*). By means of the LEN function the length of the corresponding actual argument at any time can be found.

6.1.6   Indexing

An index function is provided which works exactly as suggested in section 5.7. It is called INDEX.

```
INDEX ('INDICATE', 'CAT')   yields      5
INDEX ('SEARCH ME', 'CLUE')             0 (search fails)
INDEX ('MULTINATIONAL', 'TI')           4
```

The two arguments may be character expressions and the result is integer.

6.1.7   Reading and writing

The input/output facilities provided for strings in Fortran 77 are, as might be expected, an extension of those provided for single characters, as described in section 4.2.3. The difference is that when reading or writing a CHARACTER value with a length greater than one, the format specification must be changed from A1 to An when n is the length.

```
      CHARACTER*80 CARD
      READ (*, 300) CARD
300   FORMAT (A80)
```

This will read an 80-character record into the variable CARD. If the next input record is longer than 80 characters, the remainder of the record will be ignored. If the next input record is less than 80 characters in length, this is an error, but many implementations will pad out the record with blanks for you. Despite the multitude of facilities for input and output in Fortran 77, the programmer who simply wants to read the next record, no less and no more, is inadequately served.

Output of CHARACTER values is as one might expect:

```
      WRITE (*, 550) CARD
550   FORMAT (' ', A80)
```

6.2   Pascal

In Fortran 77 we saw that entities of type CHARACTER may hold a single character or a fixed length character string. In Pascal, on the other hand, type char is strictly for the storage of single characters. One may declare arrays of this type, eg

var str: **array** [1 .. 5] **of** char;

This permits str to hold five characters in locations str[1], str[2], ... str[5]. It is also possible to specify that the elements of the array should be packed (see section 2.2):

var str: **packed array** [1 .. 5] **of** char;

In this case it is still possible to refer to the individual locations str[1], str[2] etc, but the programmer is warned that this may take considerably more processor time than referring to elements of an unpacked array (because packing and unpacking may be needed). A packed array of char containing more than one element, whose subscripts start at 1 is said to be of 'string type'.

A character string constant takes the same form in Pascal as in Fortran 77:

> 'This is a string'
> 'That''s right'
> '0123456789'

Here again, an apostrophe within the strings is represented as two consecutive apostrophes. A character string constant is considered to be of string type, ie to be equivalent to a packed array of char containing more than one element and with its subscript starting at one.

This means that a constant with more than one character is of string type; with just one character it is of type char; and a null constant with zero characters is not permitted.

6.2.1 Assignment

Assignment between arrays of identical type is possible in Pascal. So after the declaration

var str, stg: **packed array** [1 .. 5] **of** char;

the following assignments are legal:

> str := 'ABCDE';
> stg := str;

However, the lengths of the arrays and constants must be the same. Assignment between arrays of different lengths is not permitted. Also if constants are to be assigned to arrays of char, those arrays must be packed. There is no possibility of having a more complicated string expression in the assignment statement. The examples here show the only two types of assignments possible for whole strings, assigning from an array or from a constant.

6.2.2 Comparison

The six relational operators for Pascal described in section 4.3.2 may be used between operands of string type with the same length. This allows such statements as

> **if** str = 'ABCDE' **then** ...
>
> **if** str < stg **then** ...

The operands must be packed, they must have more than one element, their subscripts must start at one and they must be of the same length. The comparison is performed from left to right on a character by character basis using the machine's collating sequence.

6.2.3 Type conversion

In Pascal, each element of an array of char is of type char, so no type conversion need be performed between a char variable and such an array element. For example:

> **var** c: char;
>
> str: **array** [1 .. 5] **of** char;
>
> pkstr: **packed array** [1 .. 5] **of** char;
>
> ...
>
> c := str[1];

Two procedures, pack and unpack, are provided for converting between packed and unpacked arrays of the same type. So, given the declarations above, the characters in unpacked form in str may be copied to a packed form in pkstr by means of the statement

> pack (str, 5, pkstr);

the second argument indicating the number of characters involved. The reverse operation, unpacking the contents of pkstr into str, can be performed by

> unpack (pkstr, str, 5);

There are no explicit facilities provided for converting numbers into strings or vice versa. Procedures can be written by the user to do this. (See exercise 1, section 6.4.)

6.2.4 Concatenation

There is no simple way to concatenate strings in Pascal. The only way a concatenated string can be built up from shorter strings is by copying the strings character by character. For example:

```
var compound: array [1 .. 6] of char;
    first, second: array [1 .. 3] of char;
    i: integer;
...
for i := 1 to 3 do compound[i] := first[i];
for i := 4 to 6 do compound[i] := second[i-3];
```

These statements will place in the array called compound the string which was in first followed by the string which was in second.

Having to resort to such methods means that even if the computer has hardware instructions for handling strings of consecutive characters, these instructions cannot be exploited for the concatenation process.

6.2.5 Substring selection

The only way to select a substring of a string in Pascal is to copy the required portion of the string, character by character. If, for instance, the following declarations have been used:

```
var whole: array [1 .. 6] of char;
    sub: array [1 .. 3] of char;
    i: integer;
```

then characters two to four of array whole may be placed in array sub by means of the statement

```
for i := 2 to 4 do sub[i-1] := whole[i];
```

6.2.6 Indexing

No means is provided for finding the index of a substring within a string. Code can be written by the programmer to do this using the facilities provided (see exercise 2, section 6.4), but once again this has to be on a character by character basis. Machine instructions which will compare packed strings cannot be used.

6.2.7 Reading and writing

Entities of string type cannot normally be read in Pascal. If an array of type char is to be read, then it is necessary to do so a character at a time (testing all the time to see whether the end of line has been reached).

It is possible to write out strings, so the following statement is permitted:

write ('Value of pkstr is:- ', pkstr);

Multiple arguments to this procedure (write) are acceptable. In this case two strings are being written out, one a constant and the other a packed array of char. They will be concatenated on the one output record, which will then be terminated after a subsequent call to procedure writeln.

6.3 Critique

Pascal is intended to be a simple language with few facilities, easy to learn and to implement. It is not surprising if it does little more than dip a toe into the pool of string processing.

Fortran 77, on the other hand, teems with facilities. There has been an attempt to provide character strings as a type. One of the major hindrances to this is the hidebound character of Fortran input/output. However, even apart from this, string processing in Fortran 77 is still inadequately provided for.

The main obstacle to the use of strings in both languages is quite simple, and should by now be clearly obvious to the reader. Character strings are by nature variable in length. The number of characters currently belonging to a particular string is part of the information. Chopping or padding the string to a predetermined length is not at all what is required. A string variable should be capable of holding the null character string, and the corresponding null string constant is a vital necessity. Being deprived of it is like trying to do arithmetic with the restriction that no value must ever turn out to be zero.

Both Fortran 77 and Pascal require one to know when writing the program just how long each string will be at execution time. When using languages which are so ill-equipped for string processing needs, the programmer has to go it alone, writing for himself the facilities which the language does not afford.

The PL/I language goes a step further in that it allows a varying length character string type. A variable of this type may be assigned strings with length from zero characters up to a maximum. This maximum length must be specified when the variable is declared, and obviously space to store the maximum length of string is reserved permanently for the variable. This is certainly a step in the right direction, and permits the use of varying length character strings, but it is still not enough. If, for instance, a large number of English words are to be accumulated and stored by the program, then reserving for each word enough space in which to store the longest would be hopelessly inefficient.

Obviously the provision of fully variable strings is a chamber of horrors from which language designers and compiler writers shrink back. In the next chapter we must explore the difficulties which must be overcome.

6.4   Exercises

For the following exercises, if you are not familiar with Pascal or Fortran 77, supplement the information given in this chapter with informal devices of your own choosing, eg for control structures.

(1)   Write a Pascal procedure to take two arguments, one an integer and the other declared as **array** [1 .. 10] **of** char. The procedure should convert the integer value into a character string.

(2)   Write a Pascal function with two arguments, declared as char arrays, the first of length 5 and the second of length 10. The function returns the index of the shorter string within the longer string, or zero if no occurrence is found.

(3)   Write Fortran 77 statements to take a variable declared as CHARACTER*80 and to reduce all sequences of blanks within its value to single blanks (except for trailing blanks at the end of the string).

7

Data structures for strings

7.1   Introduction

We need to be able to store character strings of variable length. Reserving the maximum amount of store for every variable is not acceptable. Rather, each variable should be allocated at any one time only the space needed to store its current value.

This implies that a pool of space is needed from which space can be allocated to variables as necessary. A further requirement is that space be re-used when it is no longer needed. In other words, a dynamic store allocation and retrieval system is needed.

In addition to space for the actual character strings it will be necessary to store pointers, the lengths of strings and perhaps other values. Data structures must be created for these different items. It is assumed that the reader has some familarity with data structures, especially with pointers and linked lists. See for instance Page and Wilson (1978).

Various different data structures will be considered in this chapter, and their strong and weak points examined. No structure exists which is satisfactory in every respect. The following criteria will be used when judging their suitability.

(1)   The structure should be efficient in terms of space. The overheads for pointers etc should not be excessive in comparison with the space taken up by the actual characters.

(2)   Accessing the structure should be efficient in terms of time. A corollary of this is that the characters should preferably be stored contiguously so that use can be made of machine instructions to move and compare such strings.

(3)   Character string operations should be conveniently

performed. This applies in particular to the key operations of assignment, comparison, concatenation and substring selection.

(4)   It should be possible to re-use the space allocated when it is no longer needed.

In this chapter it is assumed that the computer is a byte machine, so that the extra problems of packing and unpacking characters on a word machine may temporarily be ignored.

7.2   Contiguous strings

This is one of the simplest ways of storing strings. A continuous array of bytes is used to store the characters. We will call this array the 'character store'. Each variable has a pointer to the first character of its value, and the length of that value. Let us suppose that four string variables called text1, text2, text3 and text4 have the values "cat", "a", "would" and "sup" respectively. Then the store can be displayed like this:

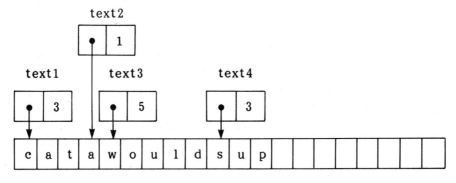

The overheads in storing a string are minimal. In addition to the characters and their length, the only extra information is one pointer. The characters are stored contiguously, so use can be made of machine instructions to compare and copy character strings.

A null string has a length of zero, in which case the value of the pointer is irrelevant.

Comparison of two strings is an easy matter. The minimum of the two lengths is found. The two strings are then compared up to this minimum length. If the strings differ in this initial comparison, then this gives the result of comparing the strings. If

60

the strings are identical up to the minimum length, then comparison between the strings is simply a comparison of their lengths.

Concatenation is performed by copying the two strings into an unused part of the the character store. A statement such as

    text3 := concat(text1, text4);

is performed in two parts. First the concatenation on the right is performed to produce a new string in the character store.

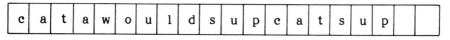

Characters 13 to 18 are the newly concatenated string. The second part of the operation is to assign this to text3, by resetting this variable's pointer and length.

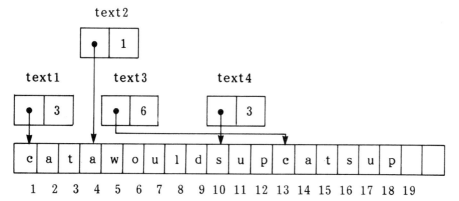

The value of text3 is now "catsup", beginning at character 13 and six characters in length.

The former value of text3, characters 5 to 9, are no longer used. No variable points to them. Can the space which they occupy be re-used? The contents of the character store could be compacted by copying them into the area which has been freed:

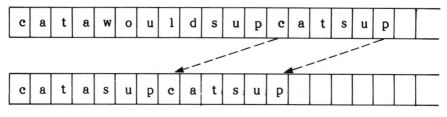

| c | a | t | a | w | o | u | l | d | s | u | p | c | a | t | s | u | p | | |

| c | a | t | a | s | u | p | c | a | t | s | u | p | | | | | | |

1 2 3 4 5 6 7 8 9 10 11 12 13 14 15 16 17 18 19

Now the first unused character is at position 14 rather than position 19, and we have gained the five characters which were lost.

The task of reorganisation is not complete, however. Variables text3 and text4 now have pointers which point to the wrong characters. It is obvious that these pointers must be updated so that they point to positions five places further to the left. Let us formulate the general rule in such a case. When part of the character store (characters x to x+n-1) is no longer needed, the characters at positions x+n and above must be moved n places to the left. At the same time, all variables must be scanned, and if their pointers are to positions higher than x, then these pointers must be reduced by n places. The situation in our example then looks like this:

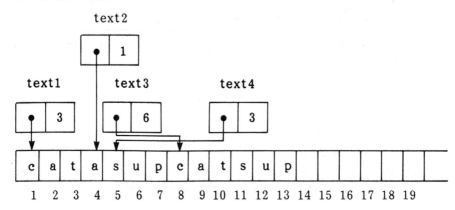

1 2 3 4 5 6 7 8 9 10 11 12 13 14 15 16 17 18 19

Although the space freed can be re-used, the cost is prohibitive. For every assignment, on average half the characters stored must be moved. In addition, every pointer must be examined and on average half of them must be updated.

Substring selection is possible with this method by means of copying the required substring to a free part of the character store. For instance, the statement

text1 := subst(text3, 2, 2);

will cause (before a further compaction of the character store) the result:

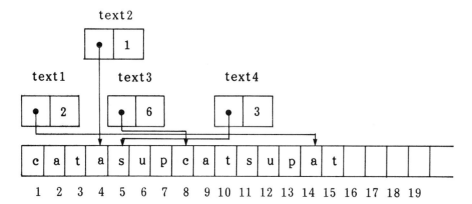

Characters one to three are now no longer in use, and a further compaction is possible. On the other hand, if compactions of the character store are not envisaged (ie the characters freed will not be re-used) then a substring selection need not copy the substring. It is possible for text1 to point at the substring "at" within the value of text3, so that the result would be

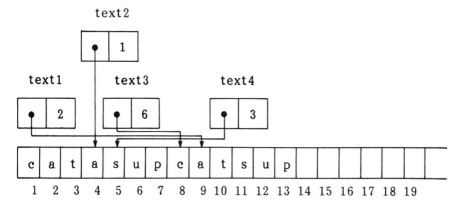

However, if text3 is assigned a different value, compaction of the character store is not possible as text1 still points to a place inside the former value of text3. The re-use of store then

becomes so complicated to organise that it is better not to attempt it.

To summarise, this method is temptingly simple, and can be efficiently implemented in every respect except for the re-use of store, which proves to be its Achilles heel.

7.3 Chained characters

This method is at the other extreme from that of contiguous strings. Each character is accompanied by its own pointer. Characters are formed into a string by means of their pointers, producing linked lists such as:

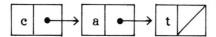

The pointer associated with 't' here is the null pointer, indicating the end of the list. The combination of a character plus its accompanying pointer will be referred to here as a 'cell'.

Variables may have associated with them a pointer to the first character of the value. If the pointer is null, then the variable has as its value the null character string. The initial values of the four variables used in the last section may then be represented as:

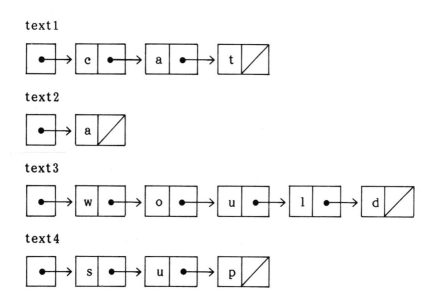

64

Comparison between two strings can be performed by means of two subsidiary pointers. Initially these pointers are set equal to the first pointers of the strings.

str1

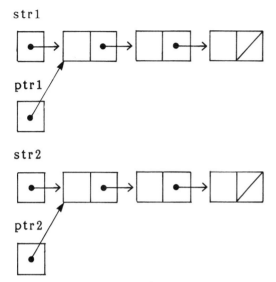

ptr1

str2

ptr2

The two strings being compared here are called str1 and str2. The pointers are called ptr1 and ptr2. The steps taken are then

(1)   If both ptr1 and ptr2 contain the null pointer, then the strings are equal.

(2)   If either ptr1 or ptr2 contains the null pointer, the corresponding string is less than the other one.

(3)   If the characters pointed to are not equal, comparison of them gives the same result as comparison between the strings.

(4)   Place in ptr1 and ptr2 the pointers of the cells to which they are currently pointing, and return to step (1).

If the first characters in str1 and str2 are equal, then after step (4) the situation will be:

str1

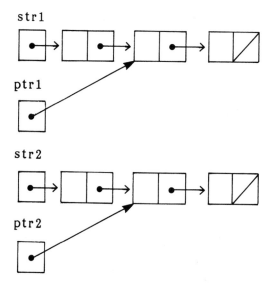

Note that it is not possible to use machine instructions which access strings of contiguous characters. With this method, no two characters are ever adjacent.

Concatenation is performed by building up a composite string by copying the component strings. Let us consider the statement

text3 := concat(text1, text4);

First a copy is made of the string value of text1, using free cells:

text1

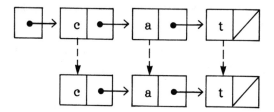

Now a copy of the string value of text4 is appended.

66

text4

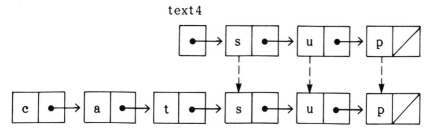

This is the string whose value is to be assigned to text3. However, first the present value of text3 must be removed. This means that the five cells currently containing the characters 'w', 'o', 'u', 'l' and 'd' are no longer needed. These cells can be chained to a special linked list comprising cells for re-use. When free cells are needed, they may be unlinked from this list. Now text3 can point to the newly constructed string.

The example here illustrates the chief virtue of this method; the cells can easily be re-used without the need for expensive compaction of store.

Substring selection is easily performed by chaining down the cells until the starting point is reached, then copying the required number of characters to form a new string.

With the method of chained characters, all string operations are easily implemented and re-use of space is achieved with great simplicity. However, there are severe drawbacks to this method. The overheads in terms of space are excessively large. Each character has an accompanying pointer which may occupy three times as much space as the character or more. In terms of execution time the method is inefficient also. Machine instructions to handle packed strings cannot be used. All operations involve chaining down the linked lists rather than directly addressing the required characters. Text processing is certainly possible by this method, but only at a price.

7.4   Chained blocks

This method is effectively a compromise between the previous two methods. Contiguous blocks of characters are chained together. Within a block the characters are adjacent. Blocks may be allocated as needed and when not in use they may be chained together for re-use.

If we suppose for the purpose of example that a block can hold four characters, then the initial situation, using the same variables as in the last two sections, will be as follows:

text1

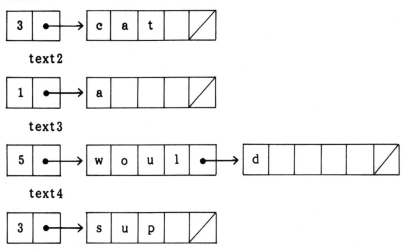

text2

text3

text4

Comparison of strings is fairly straightforward by this method. The minimum of the two lengths is taken, and comparison proceeds block by block. The last comparison may involve less than a full block. Machine instructions which compare character strings may be used within the limits of one block. If both strings are identical within the minimum length, then the comparison depends on the two lengths.

Concatenation is performed by copying the two strings in turn to build up a new string. This is not so straightforward. Once again we will consider the statement

text3 := concat(text1, text4);

A free block is acquired, and the value of text1 is copied into it.

text1

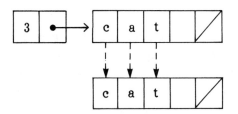

This block is not filled, so characters must be copied from the first block of text4 to fill it.

text4

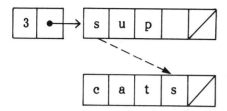

Now a further free block must be acquired, chained to the first one, and remaining characters from text4 copied over.

text4

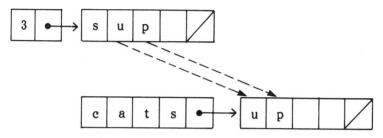

The two blocks which hold the current value of text3 must be chained into the list of cells for re-use. Now the pointer of text3 can be set to point to the first of its new blocks, and the count set equal to the sum of the counts for text1 and text4.

text3

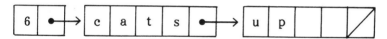

The problem occurred here when concatenating the second value on to the first, because the blocks from which the characters are copied are out of step with the blocks to which they are going.

The same problem (blocks being out of step) occurs with substring selection, as this must be performed by copying the selected substring to make a new string.

In summary, this method allows re-use of space at the expense of the space taken up by pointers. This overhead is much less than the previous method, though. Operations are somewhat more complicated. Machine instructions operating on contiguous strings are possible, but no more than one blockful of characters can be processed this way at any time, and fewer than this will be processed by one machine instruction when handling an unfilled block or when blocks get out of step.

7.5 Contiguous blocks

The method described in this section is a simplified representation of the way strings are stored in one implementation of SNOBOL4 (see Griswold, 1972).

Space is allocated in fixed-size amounts, such as a word or a double word, depending on the word length of the machine. Such a unit of space is normally used to store a 'descriptor', which will be represented here as

The first two fields of the descriptor are used for small items of information such as flags. The third field is large enough to store a pointer. The unit of space used for a descriptor may be used to store other information (eg a character string), in which case it is useful to call it still a 'descriptor', even though it is not technically one.

When a string needs to be stored, four descriptors are allocated to keep various pieces of information about the string. In addition, enough descriptors are allocated to hold the characters of the string in packed form. Let us suppose, for instance, that the string "DIAGNOSTIC" is encountered, and that a descriptor is of sufficient size to hold eight characters. Then the data structure which is created will look like this:

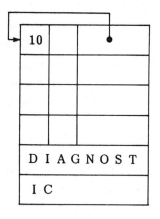

title descriptor

value descriptor

label descriptor

chain descriptor

Note that a contiguous set of descriptors is allocated. The descriptors are similar to the blocks of the previous method, but since they are adjacent there is no need to chain them together. Other descriptors may have pointers to this string, in which case they point to the title descriptor.

The first field of the title descriptor is the length of the string. The other three descriptors are needed for various purposes. For instance, DIAGNOSTIC may be the name of a variable having a value of its own, perhaps another string, in which case the value descriptor points to this string.

The characters which form the string value are packed into as many descriptors as are needed. The final descriptor may be partially unfilled.

The surprising fact here is that the pointer in the title descriptor points to itself. What need can there possibly be for such a pointer? The answer is, of course, that it does not always chase its own tail in such a way. It is used when the store needs to be compacted. But more of that in a little while.

Because the whole string is stored as contiguous characters (the boundary between descriptors having no real existence) machine instructions can be used to operate on the string in its entirety. Concatenation involves creating a new structure and copying the two strings, which is easily and efficiently performed.

For substring selection, SNOBOL4 does not create new substrings, but rather sets up a point to the target string, storing the offset of the substring (ie its distance from the start of the target string) and its length.

A problem arises when descriptors (singly or in a set) are no longer needed. It would be possible to chain them into a list for re-use, but this would not be adequate. When a string is created a set of contiguous descriptors is needed. This means that the unused descriptors must be adjacent to one another. If a string needs to be stored which is longer than any string which has been freed, there may not be any set of contiguous descriptors long enough to hold it.

Because of this, no attempt is made to reclaim unused descriptors until insufficient descriptors remain at the top of the store. At that point, the whole of the string store is compacted, so that unused descriptors are once again at the upper end of the store.

This compaction of strings is known in SNOBOL4 as 'storage regeneration', and is carried out automatically whenever it is needed. There are four steps in this process.

The first step is to mark all strings which are in use. The test of whether a string is in use is (roughly speaking) whether pointers outside the string are pointing to it. This means a test of all descriptors in certain parts of the store. The strings to which they point must be 'marked', ie a certain flag in the second field of the title descriptor is set. If a string is marked, its own descriptors must be examined to see whether they point to other strings. If they do, those other strings must also be marked, and so on. The process is obviously a recursive one.

When the marking is finished the strings which are no longer needed can be identified by the fact that their titles are not marked. It is now possible to scan through the whole store of strings, and when an unused string is encountered, to predict the position to which the next used string must be moved. This may be shown diagrammatically.

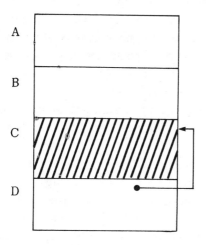

A, B, C and D represent strings (each having four descriptors plus the characters). C is no longer needed, so string D may be moved up into its place. The pointer in the title descriptor of D may now be used to point, not to itself as formerly, but to the new position for D. This is the second step in the process, called 'title adjustment'.

The third step is to scan through all descriptors which point to strings. The pointer of the descriptor is replaced by the pointer in the title descriptor of the string to which it points. If the title points to itself (which is the case still for A and B above) then the descriptor pointing to this string is left unchanged. If, however, the title now points to the new location for the string, the descriptor will be changed to point to this new location. This third step is known as 'pointer adjustment'.

The fourth and final step is 'block movement', in which the string storage is compacted, the strings being moved to their new locations. Now once again the title descriptors point to themselves.

The method of contiguous strings was censured for its need to compact the whole character store and to check all pointers. However, that was needed after every assignment. SNOBOL4 storage regeneration is only necessary when almost all the string space is exhausted. The more complicated data structure permits the store to be reorganised without having pointers coming adrift from their target strings.

7.6   Conclusion

The data structures for storing strings which have been presented in this chapter are only a sample of the possibilities. The efficient storage and processing of variable length character strings is certainly attainable, though hardly elementary. The most efficient and flexible methods usually require the most intricate data structures. The difference between general-purpose languages (such as Pascal and Fortran 77) and string-handling languages (such as SNOBOL4) is that the former leave it to the programmer to invent his own mechanisms, whereas the latter do it all for him behind the scenes.

8

Introduction to SNOBOL

8.1   SNOBOL

SNOBOL4 is a language which was developed at Bell Telephone Laboratories. It is designed to facilitate character string operations, although other types of value are also handled. It is usually implemented by means of a portable interpreter, but a compiler (SPITBOL) is also available. SNOBOL4 is, as may be imagined, the fourth in an evolutionary series of languages. As SNOBOL4 is now the established and most well-known of these languages, it is commonly referred to as SNOBOL, which will also be the practice in this book.

The syntax and philosophy of SNOBOL is different from most other programming languages, and so some time will be spent here in introducing features with many examples. Only a selection of the facilities can be described. Those interested in learning more should consult Griswold, Poage & Polonsky (1971).

8.2   Basic concepts

SNOBOL statements are usually contained in one line. It is possible to continue statements, but we will not trouble ourselves with this at the moment. If a line begins with a name (not preceded by blanks) this is the label of the statement. All programs must have as their last line a null statement with the label END:

END

If a line has no label, the line must have at least one blank character at the beginning of it. In SNOBOL, outside of strings, more than one blank is always equivalent to one blank. On the other hand, blanks are important in SNOBOL and should not be

74

added except in the positions shown.

A SNOBOL variable has a name which begins with a capital letter and is followed by any number of capital letters, digits, periods or underlines. The following are therefore legal variable names:

X
ANABOLICSTEROIDS
ANNABELLE_LEE
R1.DIVIDED.BY.R2

A variable may be assigned a value by means of an assignment statement, eg

A = 'Help!'

Note that the start of the line is left blank, showing that there is no label. The equals sign must be surrounded by blanks. A rule of SNOBOL is that all binary (or 'dyadic') operators (those which refer to operands on each side of them) must be preceded and followed by blanks. A string constant is enclosed in either single apostrophes (' ... ') or quotation marks (" ... ") and may be of any length (within the limits of one statement line, which cannot be longer than 80 characters).

The right hand side of an assignment statement may, of course, be an expression. The minimum form of such an expression is rather surprising. It is nothing at all, and the value assigned is the null string.

RES =

Now RES will have the null character string as its value.

Reading and writing are done by means of certain special variables. Whenever the value of the variable INPUT is needed, an input record is read and becomes the new value. Whenever a value is assigned to the variable OUTPUT, this value is also written out as a complete line.

It is now possible to write a complete SNOBOL program.

LN = INPUT
OUTPUT = LN
END

The first statement requires the value of INPUT, so a record is read and this string is assigned to INPUT. This same value is then assigned to OUTPUT, and at the same time is printed out. After this second statement is completed, a statement with the label END causes termination of the program. The overall effect is then that the first data card is printed out.

There is in fact no need for the auxiliary variable LN in the program. Exactly the same effect could be achieved more economically in two lines:

```
        OUTPUT  =  INPUT
END
```

Being able to read a record as a character string may appear to be completely in accordance with the requirements of section 5.8. This is not necessarily so. When SNOBOL was originally implemented, the input/output was based on Fortran. Many implementations still deal only with fixed length records, by default 80 characters long. Perhaps in this day and age there are versions of SNOBOL which will read truly variable records. Let us hope so.

Transfer of control is handled by specifying at the end of a statement the label to which control is to be transferred. This is the so-called 'goto' field, preceded by a colon. The label in this field is enclosed in parentheses. We could, for instance, change the first program above to

```
IN      LN  =  INPUT
        OUTPUT  =  LN         :(IN)
END
```

After the second statement has been performed, control is sent to the statement labelled IN once more. Since a goto may refer to its own statement, the program may be rewritten as

```
IN      OUTPUT  =  INPUT         :(IN)
END
```

Each time the first statement is completed, control returns to it once more. All the input records will be written out, but as there is no test for the end of file, execution will terminate with an error message when an attempt is made to read a non-existent record.

One of the fundamental concepts of SNOBOL is that a statement may succeed or fail. For example, a statement referring to INPUT will fail if there is no record to be read. If no such problems are encountered, the statement succeeds. The previous program may be modified to loop back only if the statement succeeds:

```
IN      OUTPUT  =  INPUT       :S(IN)
END
```

Each time a record is read and written successfully, control passes back to IN. At the end of file, an attempt to read a new record into INPUT fails. The success goto is not taken, and so control passes to the next statement in sequence, which terminates the program normally.

The goto field may specify a transfer of control in the event of a failure (using F instead of S), or both may appear together. The previous program could have been written as

```
IN      OUTPUT  =  INPUT       :S(IN)F(END)
END
```

On success control passes to IN; on failure it goes to END. The two branches can be specified in either order, so that

```
    :F(END)S(IN)
```

is just as good as

```
    :S(IN)F(END)
```

A statement terminates as soon as it fails, so that if the statement

```
    OUTPUT  =  INPUT
```

fails when trying to give INPUT a value, no assignment is performed to OUTPUT.

Concatenation of strings can readily be performed in SNOBOL, but a peculiarity of the language is that there is no explicit operator for concatenation. The two values are written separated by one or more blanks. So

```
    STRING1  =  'Note'
    STRING2  =  STRING1  ' this'
```

will assign to STRING2 the value 'Note this'. The statement

```
    CAT  =  'My '  "cat's"  ' ill'
```

will give CAT the following value:

```
    My cat's ill
```

The program which now follows will read input records and print them indented from the left of the page.

```
IN      OUTPUT  =  '              '  INPUT    :S(IN)
END
```

8.3   Numeric values

Any variable may be assigned an integer value at any time.

```
N  =  1
NUM_OF_RUNS  =  15
TEMP  =  -30
```

In the last statement there must be no blanks between the minus and the 30.   Just as in SNOBOL binary operators must be surrounded with blanks, so unary (or 'monadic') operators must be preceded, but not followed, by a blank.

Numeric expressions are permitted, in the usual way:

```
N  =  N  +  1
B  =  (N  -  TEMP)  *  12
```

A variable does not have any specified type, so it is possible to assign at different times values of various types to the same variable.

When necessary, numeric values will be changed to string type. This will be needed when a numeric value is being written out, or concatenated with a string.   For instance, after the following statements

```
N  =  83
OUTPUT  =  N
RESULT  =  N  ' degrees Fahrenheit'
```

the string value '83' will have been printed out, and RESULT will contain the value '83 degrees Fahrenheit'.

Similarly, a string value is, when necessary, converted to an integer value if this can be done.   This is necessary when the string is entering into some arithmetic operation with an integer, for instance.   If N has the value 83, then

```
N  =  N  +  '1'
```

will set N to 84.

As an example of the use of integers and strings, the following program reads a deck of cards and prints them out, numbering them.

```
        N  =  1
IN      OUTPUT  =  INPUT  N    :F(END)
        N  =  N  +  1    :(IN)
END
```

The binary operators provided for integers are:

+   addition
−   subtraction
*   multiplication
/   division
**   exponentiation

Between integers the result of division is also an integer, the value being truncated. SNOBOL supports real numbers also, but these will not be described in this book.

There are two unary operators for integers, + and -.

8.4   Primitive functions

So-called 'primitive' functions are those which are built-in as part of SNOBOL, as opposed to those written by the user.

The function SIZE takes a single character string as its argument and returns a value indicating the length of that argument. So the statement

```
FRUIT  =  'PINEAPPLE'
N  =  SIZE(FRUIT)
```

will place in N the value 9.

The function DUPL(string,integer) produces multiple copies of a string. An example is:

```
RHYTHM  =  DUPL('Bang', 4)
```

RHYTHM now contains 'BangBangBangBang'. To print out a line of asterisks one may use

```
OUTPUT  =  DUPL('*',120)
```

Many primitive functions are available in SNOBOL. A number of them are useful for pattern matching, of which more later. There is also a very important class of functions called predicates.

8.5   Predicates

Predicates are functions which return the null character string as their value. Not very useful, you may think. However, they have one other attribute. They may succeed or fail. For instance, the predicate LT takes two integer arguments. If the first argument is less than the second, then the predicate succeeds and the null character string is returned. Otherwise the predicate fails.

Let us consider the following program.

```
        ASTLINE  =  DUPL('*', 120)
        LINE  =  1
OUT     OUTPUT  =  ASTLINE
        LINE  =  LT(LINE, 10)  LINE  +  1    :S(OUT)
END
```

The first line creates a character string of 120 asterisks for use later. The second line initialises a count LINE to one. The line labelled OUT prints the line of asterisks. The next line takes LINE, adds one to the value, and invokes the predicate LT. If LINE is less than 10, the predicate succeeds and the null string is concatenated with the incremented value of LINE. This is then assigned to LINE, and as the statement succeeded, control passes back to OUT. After 10 lines of asterisks have been printed, LINE is 10, LT(LINE,10) fails, and control passes to the next statement, and the program terminates.

Besides LT, there are five other predicates which will compare pairs of integer values. These are

LE	less than or equal to
EQ	equal to
NE	not equal to
GT	greater than
GE	greater than or equal to

If strings are used as arguments to these six predicates, they will be converted to numeric form before comparison.

In addition, the predicate LGT ('lexicographically greater than') takes two string arguments and succeeds if the first one follows the second in alphabetic order.

The predicates IDENT and DIFFER take pairs of arguments of any type and test whether the arguments are identical. For our purposes, this means whether they are of the same type and are the same value. IDENT succeeds if they are identical; DIFFER succeeds if they are different. So the following function references will succeed:

```
IDENT('ABC', 'AB' 'C')
IDENT(5, 3 + 2)
DIFFER('CHALK', 'CHEESE')
DIFFER(3, '3')
```

whereas the following will fail:

```
IDENT('5', 5)
IDENT('JOY', 'SORROW')
DIFFER('ABC', 'AB' 'C')
DIFFER(0, 12/70)
IDENT('Puss', '' )
```

In the last example, the second argument was the null string. In such a case, the second argument may be omitted, ie a missing argument is taken to be the null string. Consider, for instance

```
OUTPUT = DIFFER(TEXT) TEXT
```

The value of TEXT will only be printed if it is not null. This is because DIFFER will fail if TEXT has the value null (assumed as the second argument), and in this case nothing will be assigned to OUTPUT. On the other hand, if TEXT is not null, DIFFER succeeds and its result (the null string) is concatenated before the value of TEXT and printing takes place.

The arguments to functions may be expressions, and may include references to other functions.

```
OUTPUT = GT(SIZE(TEXT), 4) TEXT
```

This will print out the value of TEXT if it is more than four characters in length.

8.6 Pattern matching

The subject of pattern matching is such an important one that a whole chapter must be devoted to it later. At the same time, it is so fundamental to the philosophy of SNOBOL that some introduction to this topic must be provided immediately.

Up to now the most complete structure of a SNOBOL statement has taken the form:

```
label    subject  =  object   :goto
```

This is not the fullest form, however. It is possible to have the structure:

label   subject   pattern   =   object   :goto

Let us take as an example the statement

LINE ' ' = '**'

The pattern here is a single blank character. The subject (here LINE) is scanned for an occurrence of the pattern. If the pattern 'matches', then the part of the subject which matches is replaced by the object (here a pair of asterisks). So if LINE originally had the value

This is a string

it will be changed to

This**is a string

Note that not every occurrence of the pattern is changed; the pattern match proceeds from left to right, and the first match stops the process. If no match is found in the whole of the subject, the statement fails.

If all blanks in LINE are to be replaced by pairs of asterisks, one could write

RB   LINE ' ' = '**'   :S(RB)

Each time a blank is successfully replaced by asterisks, control returns to the start of the statement. When no blanks remain in LINE, the statement fails and control passes to the next statement in sequence.

All the blanks in LINE may be removed by changing the statement to

RB   LINE ' ' =   :S(RB)

Here the object is (by default) the null character string. The value in LINE will be changed to

Thisisastring

The assignment part of such a pattern-matching statement is not necessary. A pattern match may be performed, not with the purpose of replacing the matched string, but simply to test to see whether such a string is present or not. The useful outcome is then whether the statement succeeds or fails. As an example, the following program prints only those input lines which contain the string 'prog'.

```
READ   LINE  =  INPUT              :F(END)
       LINE  'prog'                :F(READ)
       OUTPUT  =  LINE             :(READ)
END
```

The second line tests to see whether LINE contains 'prog'. If it
does not, the statement fails and control passes to READ. If it
does contain 'prog', the statement succeeds and the next
statement is obeyed, which prints out LINE.

8.7   Evaluation of SNOBOL so far

As SNOBOL is so different from general-purpose
languages, the aim in this chapter has been to introduce the main
features of the language in a pedagogical fashion. Now it is time
to evaluate what has been revealed so far, and see how the basic
operations of Chapter 5 have been supplied by SNOBOL.

Assignment of strings is easily performed, and no limit is placed
on the length of the string contents of any variable. A string
constant must be contained within one 80-character line, but
longer strings may be produced by concatenation.

Comparison may be performed by means of the predicates
IDENT and DIFFER (to test for equality of strings) or LGT (in the
case of inequality). Although all needed comparisons can be
performed, the mechanisms to do this are hardly regular. This
situation contrasts with the six predicates available for comparing
numeric values.

Type conversion is readily achieved, mostly automatically. A
function CONVERT is provided for explicit type conversion,
though this has not yet been introduced here.

Concatenation is one of the main features of SNOBOL. It was
an unfortunate decision to implement it without an explicit
operator, however.

Substring selection and indexing are possible, but involve pattern
matching in ways which have not yet been described. These will
be covered in the next chapter.

Reading and writing are tailored to the needs of string
processing, with the exception noted before, that input is basically
for fixed length records only.

So the basic operations are all provided. But SNOBOL also supplies many high level operations which other languages could not attempt to approach.

8.8   Exercises

Write SNOBOL programs to do the following:

(1)   Read a deck of cards and print each card twice.

(2)   Read cards, reduce multiple blanks to single blanks and print the resulting strings (cf exercise 6.4 (3)).

(3)   Read a deck of cards and print out the number of non-blank characters on each card.

(4)   Read a deck of cards and print out each card which has at least five non-blank characters on it.

(5)   Read pairs of numbers (one per card), add them up and print out the two numbers and their sum (on the same line). Do this until you run out of cards.

(6)   Read a Fortran program and print it out with a line of asterisks printed after each subprogram. (Each Fortran subprogram is terminated by a line containing only the letters 'E', 'N' and 'D' in that order, but there may be an indefinite number of blanks before and after each of these letters. Ignore the possibility of a continuation line which may also fit this criterion.)

9

Pattern matching

The greatest part of SNOBOL is the range of facilities for pattern matching, and the most complicated part of every program is normally the application of patterns to strings. The description here is of necessity incomplete. Those who wish to learn more and to discover how a pattern match proceeds should consult Griswold, Poage & Polonsky (1971).

9.1.   Concatenation and alternation

In the previous chapter, the pattern being matched was simply a character string. This may be specified as a constant or as a variable, so that

```
STR  =  ' '
LINE  STR  =  '**'
```

is equivalent to

```
LINE  ' '  =  '**'
```

The pattern may be an expression, including concatenation. If, for instance, the variable N has the value 3, then

```
ST 'Line ' N  =  'Home'
```

will change the first occurrence of 'Line 3' within ST to 'Home'. Note carefully that the blank between ST and 'Line ' indicates the transition from the subject to the pattern, whereas the blank between 'Line ' and N is the concatenation operator.

An operator which may only be used within patterns is the alternation operator, meaning 'or'.

```
ST 'one' | 'two'  =
```

This will remove from ST the string 'one' or the string 'two', depending on which of these two strings is found first.

9.2   Pattern as a type

A pattern may be stored in a variable for use later in the pattern field of a statement. So

PAT   =   'cat' | 'dog'

stores in PAT a pattern which will match either the string 'cat' or the string 'dog'.   Then

STR   =   'The cat sat on the mat'
STR   PAT   =   'quadruped'

will change STR to contain

'The quadruped sat on the mat'

There are some primitive functions which return a pattern as their result.   For instance, the function ANY takes a character string argument and returns a pattern which will match any of the individual characters in the string.   So

ANY ('AEIOU')

is the same as writing the pattern

'A' | 'E' | 'I' | 'O' | 'U'

and the statement

LOOP   STR   ANY('AEIOUaeiou')   =   '-'   :S(LOOP)

will replace all vowels in STR with hyphens.

The function LEN takes an integer argument and returns a pattern which will match that number of characters (no matter what characters they may be).   So the statement

CARD   '('   LEN(5)   ')'   =

will remove the first occurrence of five characters surrounded by parentheses, so that if CARD originally contained

AB(CDE)FG(HIJKL)MNOP

it will after the execution of this statement have the value

AB(CDE)FGMNOP

The first character of a string may be removed by means of the statement

STR   LEN(1)   =

This statement will fail if STR initially contains the null string.

9.3   Pattern expressions

In SNOBOL a pattern is a type which permits very complex expressions. As with most expressions, parentheses may be used to group items together. For example, both alternation and concatenation are possible within the same pattern, and perentheses can be used to specify the grouping. The pattern

('L' | 'BR') ('A' | 'E') 'D'

will match the strings 'LAD', 'LED', 'BRAD' and 'BRED'. Note that this pattern includes two alternation operators and two concatention operators.

When a pattern will match any of a number of different strings, the need arises to be able to record which string has been found. For this purpose the conditional value assignment operator is used. This is a period (or full stop or decimal point) used as a dyadic operator (so it must be surrounded by blanks). It is preceded by a pattern and followed by a variable. If the pattern is successfully matched, the string matching the pattern is copied into the variable. For example

ST   ('one' | 'two') . NUM   =

will cause the first occurrence of 'one' or 'two' within ST to be deleted, and if such a string is found, a copy of it will be placed in NUM. If ST initially has the value

Stone the crows

then after the statement has been executed ST will have the value

St the crows

and NUM will contain the string 'one'. Note that it is because of the equals sign that 'one' is removed from ST. Without the equals sign, the value of ST would remain unchanged, but 'one' would still be assigned to NUM.

The conditional value assignment operator may be used to assign part of a matched pattern. This can be controlled by parentheses. The pattern

PAT = (('L' | 'BR') . A ('A' | 'E') . V 'D') . W

can be applied in a statement such as

CRD   PAT = 'ING'

If CRD originally contained

AN ADDLED EGG

then PAT will match 'LED', CRD will be changed to

AN ADDING EGG

and A will have the value 'L', V will have 'E' and W will have 'LED'.

Now we have enough equipment to perform substring selection. In section 5.5 the following example was given of such a selection:

t := substr("ABCDEF", 3, 2)

which takes the substring of "ABCDEF" from position 3, of length 2 characters, so assigning "CD" to it. Let us make this more general:

t := substr(str, i, j)

This takes the substring of str starting from character position i, j characters long. The effect of this statement is achieved in SNOBOL by means of the statement

STR   LEN(I - 1) LEN(J) . T

The subject here is STR. A character string of length I - 1 precedes the substring. Following this, a substring of length J characters is assigned to T, provided that such a substring exists. If it does not, the statement will fail and the value of T will be unchanged.

Another useful operator within patterns is the cursor position operator. This is the unary operator @. It stores in the following variable the position at which a match is being attempted. For instance, if S contains the string 'HEADING', the statement

S @POSN 'DIN'

will attempt to match 'DIN' first at the beginning of the string 'HEADING', then one character to the right and so on until a match is found. This is handled by means of a pointer or cursor, which indicates the position within the string at which this part of the pattern is being applied. The value of the cursor is assigned to the variable, so POSN will successively be given the values 0, 1, 2, 3 until the match is successful. In this case the final value of POSN represents the index of the subxstring 'DIN' within the string 'HEADING'. If the pattern does not match, POSN will continually be incremented as different positions are tried. The resulting value left in POSN will be meaningless, so it is necessary to test whether the match succeeded, and only to use the value assigned by the cursor position operator if this is so.

As an example of the use of cursor positions, here is a program to underline the first occurrence on each line of the strings 'PASCAL', 'FORTRAN' or 'LISP'.

```
       PAT = @ST 'PASCAL' ! 'FORTRAN' ! 'LISP' @FN
IN     LINE  =  INPUT                    :F(END)
       LINE  PAT                         :S(UNDR)
       OUTPUT  =  LINE                   :(IN)
UNDR   OUTPUT  =  LINE
       OUTPUT = DUPL(' ',ST) DUPL('-', FN - ST):(IN)
END
```

The whole pattern is stored in PAT for convenience. The pattern will set a cursor position in ST to show the start of the matched name, and another in FN to show the end of the name. If the pattern does not match the line read in, the line is simply printed out. If the pattern does match, control passes to UNDER, where the line is printed out followed by underlining. The first call to DUPL generates enough blanks to precede the underlined portion. The difference between FN and ST gives the length of the matched word, showing the number of underline characters needed. If the input data cards are

TESTS ON FORTRAN AND PASCAL SHOW
THAT LISP HAS MORE PARENTHESES

the printed output will appear as

TESTS ON FORTRAN AND PASCAL SHOW
        - - - - - - -
THAT LISP HAS MORE PARENTHESES
     - - - -

Constructions such as @ST and @FN do not affect the pattern matching. In effect, they will match the null character string.

Use of the cursor position operator enables a substring to be located within a string, provided that a test is made for failure of the match. This provides the indexing operation of section 5.7, and completes the set of basic operations for SNOBOL.

9.4   More pattern functions

SNOBOL provides a large number of primitive functions
for use in pattern matching. Some of the most useful of these
are described here.

So far we have had the function LEN, which matches a given
number of characters anywhere within the string, and the @
operator which records the cursor position, ie the character
position within the string at which the current part of the pattern
is being applied. There is also a function POS which fails unless
the cursor position is as specified. So, for instance

> STR   POS(0)   'cat'

will only succeed if the string 'cat' appears as the first three
characters of the string STR. Similarly

> STR   POS(15)   '='

will only succeed if the sixteenth character within STR is the
equals sign.

The function RPOS specifies the cursor position from the right
hand end of the string. The statement

> STR   '*'   RPOS(0)   =

will delete an asterisk from STR if it is the final character. The
same effect could have been accomplished by

> STR   RPOS(1)   '*'   =

The function ANY (as described in section 9.2) will match any
of a set of single characters. The function SPAN goes one better
than this; it will match any number of characters drawn from a
specified set. This means that

> SPAN('0123456789')

will match any stretch containing only numeric digits. What is
more SPAN always matches the longest sequence possible. SPAN
must match at least one character or it fails. An example of the
use of this function is to remove all punctuation marks from the
beginning of a string so as to ensure that the string starts with a
non-punctuation character:

> STR   POS(0)   SPAN(' .,:;"!?' "()")   =

The argument to SPAN is here two concatenated strings, one of
which specifies " and the other includes '.

BREAK is the reverse of SPAN. It matches the longest string of characters none of which is drawn from the specified set. So if we define punctuation marks as

PUNC = ' .,:;"!?' "()"

we may then remove the next word from a line of text by

LINE POS(0) SPAN(PUNC) BREAK(PUNC) . W =

Here SPAN skips over punctuation marks at the start of LINE. BREAK then matches all non-punctuation characters up to but not including another punctuation. This string is assigned to W. Finally everything which matched the pattern (both SPAN and BREAK) within LINE is replaced by the null string.

BREAK must find a character within its specified set (a 'break' character) or it fails. Coupled with the fact that SPAN must match at least one character, this means that in the previous example LINE must contain a string starting with at least one punctuation mark, having at least one non-punctuation character, which is followed by at least one further punctuation character. Otherwise the statement will fail.

BREAK and SPAN both have a subtle but important restriction. If either function succeeds but a subsequent part of the pattern fails, the function will not allow the cursor to be moved on to try a match somewhere else.

For example, if STR has been assigned a value by the statement

STR = 'THIS IS,A.STRING'

then in the statement

STR ANY(' ,.') 'A'

the function ANY will first succeed when the cursor is at the blank. However, the next character in STR is 'I', and so 'A' in the pattern will not match. The pattern match then backtracks and ANY allows the cursor to move on to the comma, when the whole pattern matches. If, however, the statement had been

STR SPAN(' ,.') 'A'

then when SPAN matches the blank and 'A' does not match, SPAN will not allow the cursor to be moved on, so the whole statement fails.

A very common requirement is to strip words one at a time from input lines. The following program reads data cards and prints words from the cards one per line.

```
         PUNC  =  ' .,:;"!?'  "(')"
         PAT  =  BREAK(PUNC) . WORD  SPAN(PUNC)
GET      LINE  =  INPUT  ' '                        :F(END)
         LINE  POS(0)  SPAN(PUNC)  =
STRIP    LINE  PAT  =                               :F(GET)
         OUTPUT  =  WORD                            :(STRIP)
END
```

The pattern set up this time first selects a word and then skips any punctuation characters following it. The line labelled GET reads a card and concatenates a blank to it, so that the last word on the line will be certain to have a punctuation mark after it. The next line removes punctuations before the first word. If this statement fails it is because no such punctuations are present, and no harm is done. The line labelled STRIP applies the pattern PAT. If a word is found, this is placed in WORD. The word and punctuation following it are removed from LINE. Finally WORD is printed out and control returns to STRIP. If the last word has been stripped from LINE, all punctuations following it have gone too, so LINE contains the null character string. Although BREAK will match a null string, SPAN will not, so the statement fails and control returns to GET to read another card.

9.5   Exercises

(1)   In SNOBOL, operations on strings work from left to right. In order to carry out these same operations from right to left, the easiest method is to reverse the string. Write statements to reverse the string contents of STR, so that, for instance, if STR contains 'PERHAPS' this is changed to 'SPAHREP'.

(2)   Write a program to count how many words occur in the input. (Define a word as a non-null string bounded by punctuation marks or the start or end of a line.)

10

SNOBOL arrays and tables

10.1   Arrays

In SNOBOL an array is created by a primitive function ARRAY. In its simplest form, this function takes one integer argument.

        A = ARRAY(15)

This will make A an array with 15 elements which may be referred to as A<1>, A<2>, ... A<15>.

An element of an array may be assigned a value of any type. There is nothing to prevent different elements of one array from having values of different types:

        A<1> = 'A string'
        A<2> = -25
        A<3> = ('cat' | 'dog') . A<4>

If a subscript for an array falls outside the range specified to the ARRAY function which created it, the array reference fails. This means that a loop such as the following could be used to set all the elements of an array to the same value:

```
        N  =  1
INIT    A<N>  =  35                          :F(OUT)
        N  =  N  +  1                        :(INIT)
OUT
```

There is no need to test the value of N, because when N is 16 the statement labelled INIT will fail.

There is an easier way to initialise all elements of an array to the same value. A second argument for ARRAY specifies the value to be given to each element of the array. The effect of the previous loop could have been achieved by means of the

93

statement:

    A   =   ARRAY(15, 35)

If the second argument is omitted, the null character string is assumed, which is then the value given to each element of the array.

Two-dimensional arrays can also be created. The limits on both dimensions must be specified by the first argument to ARRAY, so in this case the first argument must be a character string with the limits separated by a comma.

    YEAR   =   ARRAY('7,52', 'HOLIDAY')

YEAR will be an array with 7 x 52 elements, each element initially containing the string 'HOLIDAY'. Elements may be addressed as, for instance, YEAR<1,1> or YEAR<7,52>.

The next example uses a one-dimensional array. The problem is to count how many times each of the capital letters appears in the input text. Here is the program to do this.

```
        ALPHABET  =  'ABCDEFGHIJKLMNOPQRSTUVWXYZ'
        COUNT  =  ARRAY(26, 0)
READ    LINE  =  INPUT                              :F(TOTL)
GETC    LINE  LEN(1) . CHAR  =                      :F(READ)
        ALPHABET  CHAR  @INDEX                      :F(GETC)
        COUNT<INDEX>  =  COUNT<INDEX> + 1           :(GETC)
TOTL    N  =  1
LOOP    ALPHABET LEN(1) . LETTER  =
        OUTPUT = LETTER ' OCCURS ' COUNT<N> ' TIMES'
        N  =  LT(N,26)  N  +  1                     :S(LOOP)
END
```

The first line sets up in ALPHABET the list of capital letters. This will be used later in the program to find out which capital letter has been encountered. The second line creates an array called COUNT with 26 elements, which will be used for keeping the counts for the letters. The second argument to ARRAY specifies that each of the elements of COUNT will initially contain an integer zero. If no second argument had been used, an element which is never incremented would still contain a null character string.

The line labelled READ gets the next data record into LINE, and branches to TOTL when the input is exhausted. The line labelled GETC takes the first character of LINE, places it in CHAR, and removes this character from LINE. If LINE contains no more characters, the statement fails and control passes back to read another line. Next the character in CHAR is matched against the capital letters, stored in ALPHABET. If CHAR does not match, then CHAR does not contain a capital letter, and control returns to GETC to get another character. If CHAR does match, the cursor position immediately following the match is placed in INDEX. This means, for instance, that if CHAR contains 'A', the match will succeed at the beginning of ALPHABET, and the cursor position immediately following the first letter is 1. In this way the value placed in INDEX will represent the index value of the capital letter within CHAR, so that INDEX will contain 1 for 'A', 2 for 'B', 3 for 'C' etc. The next statement increments the appropriate COUNT element and returns to get the next character from LINE.

When control passes to TOTL, a loop produces 26 lines of output, each line printing out the next letter (stripped from ALPHABET) and the appropriate count of how many times this letter has occurred.

10.2   Indirect reference

Although this subject is not immediately connected with SNOBOL arrays and tables, it is pedagogically convenient to introduce it here.

Let us consider the previous example once more. A count needs to be kept showing the number of occurrences of the capital letters A, B, C etc. We kept these counts in the array elements COUNT<1>, COUNT<2>, COUNT<3> etc, so it was necessary to map A, B, C ... into the integers 1, 2, 3 ... in order to have subscripts for COUNT. However, A, B and C are valid SNOBOL variable names. A possibility is to store the counts in these variables, so that, for instance, the variable Q contains the number of times the letter 'Q' has been found in the input.

This can be done by means of the unary operator $. The use of this operator can be mind-boggling, so careful attention is needed at this point. When $ is applied to an item, the character string contents of that item are treated as the name of a variable. This means that

```
MID   =   'XYZ'
$MID  =   3
```

will set the value of variable XYZ to be 3.

In terms of the previous example, if CHAR has been assigned the value 'A', then a reference to $CHAR will be the same as a reference to the variable whose name is A. The program can therefore be rewritten as follows.

```
        ALPHABET   =   'ABCDEFGHIJKLMNOPQRSTUVWXYZ'
READ    LINE   =   INPUT                          :F(TOTL)
GETC    LINE   LEN(1) . CHAR   =                  :F(READ)
        ALPHABET   CHAR                           :F(GETC)
        $CHAR   =   $CHAR + 1                      :(GETC)
TOTL    N   =   1
LOOP    ALPHABET LEN(1) . LETTER   =
        OUTPUT = LETTER ' OCCURS ' $LETTER ' TIMES'
        N   =   LT(N,26)   N   +   1               :S(LOOP)
END
```

This program is almost identical to the previous one. However, there is no call to the ARRAY function to create an array, the cursor position is not stored when CHAR is matched against the alphabet, and wherever the first program had a reference to COUNT<something> the new program uses $something instead.

The variable which is accessed by means of the indirect reference operator $ does not need to have a name which follows the rules laid down in section 8.2. Any string will do, except the null string. The statement

```
'+-='   =   3
```

is invalid because it breaks the rules of syntax for SNOBOL. It is not possible to assign a value to a literal string (between apostrophes). It is, however, possible to assign a value to a variable with the name +-= as the following statements show:

```
NAME   =   '+-='
$NAME  =   3
```

In fact, this could have been done in one statement:

```
$'+-='   =   3
```

In SNOBOL every string is stored in such a way that it can

96

function as a variable and have a value of its own. In fact, every string is stored only once, in a form irrespective of the way it has been used. The assignment to YEAR of an array in the last section did not therefore create 7x52 copies of the string 'HOLIDAY', but only one, which serves for every string with this value and also for the variable with this name.

10.3   Tables

In section 10.1 the frequency of capital letters was determined by using an array called COUNT. In order to access this array, each capital letter had to be mapped into an integer representing the location within the array (the 'subscript').

In section 10.2 each capital letter was used as a variable name. It was not necessary to map this into a number. Or was it? Every addressable location in a computer has a numeric address. When we say that the variable A does not need to be mapped into a number, we mean that we do not need to do it. It is the work of compilers, interpreters and assemblers (in other words, language processors) to map the names of variables (in character string form) into unique numeric values indicating the locations at which the values of those variables are stored.

What really happened in section 10.2 was that the SNOBOL system took a character string (the contents of CHAR or LETTER) and mapped this into a location within the whole of the available store. We can summarise the mechanisms used in the previous two sections as:

(a)   Use an integer to give a location within a limited space;

(b)   Use a string to give a location within the whole store.

The third mechanism which will be used in this section can be summarised as:

(c)   Use a string to give a location within a limited space.

The 'limited space' of (a) is of course an array. The 'limited space' of (c) is called a table. A table is created by means of the TABLE function. No arguments need be given, but parentheses are still needed to indicate that it is a function call rather than a reference to a variable.

REC   =   TABLE()

After this statement has been executed, one may assign values to, for instance, REC<'A'> or to REC<'hippopotamus'> or to REC<'4'> or to REC<4>. Note that the last two are different elements of REC. The subscript need not be a string, and integers are not translated into character strings before the mapping takes place.

How many elements can be accessed? The ARRAY function required a limit to be specified which determined the size of the array. Tables are not as restrictive as this. Each time an element is referred to for the first time, that element is created. Initially the table is given a fixed size, but if more elements are needed, the size is extended. You need not worry about the details, as SNOBOL takes care of it all.

The program of the previous two sections can be rewritten once more, this time using a table called TAB.

```
          ALPHABET  =  'ABCDEFGHIJKLMNOPQRSTUVWXYZ'
          TAB  =  TABLE()
READ      LINE  =  INPUT                             :F(TOTL)
GETC      LINE  LEN(1) . CHAR  =                      :F(READ)
          ALPHABET  CHAR                             :F(GETC)
          TAB<CHAR>  =  TAB<CHAR> + 1                 :(GETC)
TOTL      N  =  1
LOOP      ALPHABET LEN(1) . LETTER  =
          TAB<LETTER>  =  IDENT(TAB<LETTER>)  0
          OUTPUT = LETTER ' OCCURS ' TAB<LETTER> ' TIMES'
          N  =  LT(N,26) N  +  1                      :S(LOOP)
END
```

Note the line immediately after the one labelled LOOP. If a certain letter (say 'Z') has not been found in the input, then the corresponding element of TAB (ie TAB<'Z'>) has not yet been created or initialised. As soon as it is referred to it will be given the null string as its value. This statement checks to see whether it does have this value, and if it does it is assigned a zero.

You may object that a table was not really needed here, and you would be right. Instead of mapping the letters into the table TAB, we could have mapped them by means of the indirect reference operator $ into the whole store, and still retrieve them satisfactorily. The program of section 10.2 has not been improved by using a table.

However, there are situations where a table is needed. In the example above, we knew what strings had been used to access the table, as these were drawn from the set of capital letters. At the end of the program the counts could be retrieved using these letters. Now let us suppose that instead of the capital letters, the program was keeping a count of how many times each word occurred in the input. When the results are to be printed out, it is impossible to generate every English word to see what its count is. How then can we find out what elements of the table have been created, and what subscripts were used?

The solution lies with another function called CONVERT. This provides explicit type conversion from one type of value to another. The first argument is the item whose type is to be converted, and the second argument specifies the type to which it is to be changed. A table may be converted to the type 'ARRAY'. Let us suppose that the following statements have been executed:

```
REC   =   TABLE()
REC<'A'>  =  15
REC<'hippoptamus'>   =   'enormous'
REC<1>  =  'no.'
A   =   CONVERT(REC, 'ARRAY')
```

Three elements of REC have been referenced. The final statement will make A a two-dimensional array (3 x 2) with the following values:

A<1,1> = 'A'		A<1,2> = 15
A<2,1> = 'hippopotamus'		A<2,2> = 'enormous'
A<3,1> = 1		A<3,2> = 'no.'

Element A$\langle$n,1$\rangle$ contains the subscript for the nth reference to the table, and A$\langle$n,2$\rangle$ contains the value stored at that place in the table.

10.4   Compiling an index

This section contains a longer example on the use of tables. A program is to be written to compile an index for a book. Data cards for this will have the index item at the start, with a colon and a page number somewhere further along the card, eg

```
steam    :15
branch lines      :17
diesel :23
branch lines       :23
steam       :24
signals       :26
```

The object of the program is to accumulate all references to the same index item and to print the items in alphabetical order, with the references separated by commas. The data above would give rise to the following output:

```
branch lines 17, 23
diesel 23
signals 26
steam 15, 24
```

The program will have three parts:

(a)   reading cards and accumulating page numbers for each item;

(b)   sorting the items into alphabetical order;

(c)   printing the items with their page number references.

Let us now look at each of these three parts in more detail.

(a)   A table will obviously be needed. The index item will be used as the subscript, and page numbers will be concatenated on to the value.

(b)   The table will need to be converted into an array. A bubble sort (or ripple sort) will be used to put the items into alphabetical order. For those not familiar with this method, a bubble sort compares adjacent items, exchanging those which are out of order. The whole array is swept through until no more exchanges need be made.

(c)   Starting from the beginning of the array, each item is output followed by its list of page numbers.

Comments in SNOBOL have an asterisk in column 1; blank lines are also permitted. To supplement the comments, fuller explanations will be interspersed with each section of the program. Here is the first section.

```
* INITIALISE
      INDEX  =  TABLE()
* ACCUMULATE ENTRIES
READ  LINE  =  INPUT                               :F(SORT)
      LINE  BREAK(':') . ITEM  SPAN(': ')  =
      ITEM  =  TRIM(ITEM)
      INDEX<ITEM> = INDEX<ITEM> ', ' TRIM(LINE)  :(READ)
```

A table is created with the name INDEX. Each data card is read into LINE. When there are no more data cards, control passes to the start of the next section. LINE is broken up, everything up to but not including the colon being put into ITEM. Colons and spaces are skipped over. All these items which are matched are removed from LINE, leaving LINE containing the page number and any following blanks. ITEM now contains the index item followed by an indeterminate number of blanks. TRIM is a useful function which removes from a string all trailing blanks (ie those at the end of the string). The final statement in this section concatenates the trimmed page number into the appropriate part of the table. Note that when an index item is encountered for the first time, an unwanted comma will be inserted before the first page number. This will need to be removed later.

```
* SORT THE ITEMS
SORT  INDEX  =  CONVERT(INDEX, 'ARRAY')
SCAN  EXCHANGE  =  'NO'
      N  =  1
COMP  LGT(INDEX<N + 1,1>, INDEX<N,1>)            :S(INCR)
      IDENT(INDEX<N + 1,1>, INDEX<N,1>)          :S(INCR)
      TEMP  =  INDEX<N + 1,1>                     :F(TOP)
      INDEX<N + 1,1>  =  INDEX<N,1>
      INDEX<N,1>  =  TEMP
      TEMP  =  INDEX<N + 1,2>
      INDEX<N + 1,2>  =  INDEX<N,2>
      INDEX<N,2>  =  TEMP
      EXCHANGE  =  'YES'
INCR  N  =  N + 1                                 :(COMP)
TOP   IDENT(EXCHANGE,'YES')                       :S(SCAN)
```

First of all the table in INDEX must be converted into an array. Since we do not need the table any more, the array may be stored under the name INDEX. Now INDEX contains a two-dimensional array, each INDEX<n,1> containing an index item and INDEX<n,2> containing the list of page number references. A bubble sort is now used to sort the array into alphabetical order of index items. Repeated scans are made through the array. N is used to keep the position within the array. Each time items N and N + 1 are not in alphabetical order, they are exchanged (together with their page references). TEMP is used as a temporary store for this exchange. EXCHANGE holds the character string 'YES' or 'NO' to indicate whether an exchange has taken place during this scan.

The statement labelled COMP branches to INCR if item N + 1 follows item N alphabetically. However, if the items are identical, LGT will fail, and we are in danger of exchanging this pair of items every time round the loop for ever. This is averted by the next statement, which uses IDENT to test for this eventuality.

The statement COMP and its successor may fail for either of two reasons. It may be that adjacent items are in the wrong order, in which case LGT fails. Alternatively, it may be that there are only N items in the array, in which case reference to INDEX<N + 1,1> will fail. In the latter case the next assignment statement will also fail, since it also includes reference to INDEX<N + 1,1>. If it fails, a branch is made to TOP, the end of the scan. At TOP, if EXCHANGE has the value 'YES', at least one exchange has been made, and control returns to SCAN to start another scan. If no exchanges have been made, control passes to the next section.

The statement labelled TOP has a peculiarity. The function call to IDENT appears within the subject field. This is quite acceptable; if the call succeeds the subject is the null string.

Note that the bubble sort is not the most efficient method of sorting; nor is the above coding the most efficient way of implementing this sort. Efficiency has here been sacrificed for the sake of simplicity.

```
* REMOVE LEADING COMMAS
        N  =  1
LOP     INDEX<N,2>  LEN(1)  =              :F(PRINT)
        N  =  N  +  1                      :(LOP)
```

As mentioned earlier, each list of page numbers starts with an unwanted comma (followed by a blank) at the start. This loop trims off the first character (the comma) leaving the blank. The statement LOP will fail when N is outside the array, and control then passes to the next section.

```
* PRINT INDEX
PRINT N  =  1
PUT   OUTPUT  =  INDEX<N,1>  INDEX<N,2>     :F(END)
      N  =  N  +  1                         :(PUT)
END
```

Finally, the index is printed, each line containing the index item followed by its page number reference.

Perhaps it may be considered one of the major triumphs of text over numbers, that one may even use strings as subscripts. However, it must be admitted that in most cases it is necessary to revert to a form in which numeric subscripts are used in order to print out the results.

10.5   Exercises

(1)   Write a program to read English text typed on cards and to print out how many words have been found with lengths 1, 2, 3, ... 20 characters.

(2)   Modify (1) to print a histogram (bar-chart) of the results. (Hint: print the bars from left to right, assuming that no bar will be longer than a print line.)

(3)   Write a program to read English text and to compile a list of all words with lengths greater than six characters. Your program should only print each such word once.

11
Word frequency count

11.1   The problem

In this chapter and the next, two larger examples will be considered in relation to the three languages, Fortran 77, Pascal and SNOBOL. In this chapter the subject will be the compilation of a frequency count for words.

First the data must be defined. It will be assumed that data records contain English text. A 'word' will be defined as any string of characters not including a punctuation mark and wholly contained within one record. Punctuation marks will be defined as comprising blanks, periods (full stops), commas or parentheses.

The output required will be kept simple in order to reduce the size of the sample programs. The requirement will be that each line of the output will show an integer indicating the number of times a word has occurred, and then the word itself. The output may then appear as follows:

```
5 IN
9 THE
3 COUNTRY
...
```

For each of the programming languages, the program will naturally fall into two parts:

(1)   Read the text, divide into words and update the counts.

(2)   Print out the counts and words stored.

11.2   Fortran 77

As Fortran 77 is limited in its support for character strings, we need to consider what resources are needed for this task. When writing the program it cannot be foreseen how many

104

different words will be encountered in the data, nor how large the longest one will be. We must allow sufficient space for a large number of words, but to reserve a maximum number of characters for each of these would be very wasteful. Each word should occupy enough space in which to store it and no more.

We must therefore consider implementing one of the data structures described in Chapter 7. Naturally we do not want to code a more complicated scheme than is necessary. There is one factor which simplifies our choice of data structure. This is the fact that no mechanism is needed for deleting strings. Once a new word is found it should be stored until the time for printing it out at the end of the run. The method of contiguous strings, described in section 7.2, is easy to implement and is efficient in every respect except for the re-use of store (which is not needed here). So this is the method to use.

A long vector is needed in which to hold the list of words. For each word we will need an indication of where that string lies within the vector, and a count of how many times it has been found so far. Fortran 77 substring selection works by specifying the starting and ending positions within the string, not the length, so it will be most convenient for us to store these two values.

The data structure will therefore be constructed from four vectors. One (which will be called CH) stores the words end-to-end. Another (called START) stores the indices of the initial characters of the words within CH, and a third vector (called TERM) stores the indices of the final characters. The fourth vector (called COUNT) stores the number of times each word has been found. So the data structure for word I will take the form:

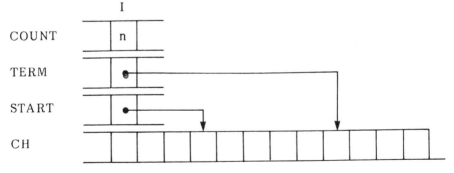

In order to give fuller documentation than would be possible with comment lines, parts of the program are interspersed with paragraphs of description.

```
PARAMETER (MAXCH=500, MAXWD=1000, NPUNC=5)
CHARACTER*(MAXCH) CH
CHARACTER*80 LINE
CHARACTER PUNC(NPUNC)
INTEGER START(MAXWD), TERM(MAXWD)
INTEGER COUNT(MAXWD)
DATA NCH /0/, NWDS /0/
DATA PUNC /' ', '.', ',', '(', ')'/
```

The PARAMETER statement defines numerical values which will not change during the execution of the program (ie constants). These constants may then be used in place of literal values.

The CH vector is defined as a single CHARACTER variable of length 500 characters. (The parentheses around MAXCH in the CHARACTER statement are necessary because of the syntax of Fortran.) Similarly LINE, used as a buffer for the input record, is a single variable capable of holding 80 characters. This is done so that we can refer to substrings of these two variables, which would not be possible if they were arrays.

The DATA statement stores initial values in variables. NCH is the count of characters which have already been stored within CH and NWDS is the number of different words which these comprise. PUNC is the set of punctuation characters, NPUNC in number.

```
10    READ (*, 20, END=130) LINE
20    FORMAT(A80)
```

It is assumed that the input records are all 80 characters long. Words are found by alternating between (a) skipping punctuation marks and (b) skipping non-punctuation characters.

```
C  SKIP PUNCTUATION MARKS
      IFIN = 0
30    DO 50 IBEGIN = IFIN+1, 80
         DO 40 I = 1, NPUNC
40          IF (LINE(IBEGIN:IBEGIN) .EQ. PUNC(I)) GO TO 50
         GO TO 60
50       CONTINUE
      GO TO 10
```

IFIN is used to mark the end of the last word found. At the start of LINE, IFIN is initialised to zero. The statement labelled 30 is the first example you have had of a DO statement. It may be paraphrased as 'Do all the statements up to the one labelled 50 repeatedly, with IBEGIN initially set to IFIN+1 and then taking successive values up to 80'. In order to show the structure of the program a little more clearly, the statements up to the end of a DO-loop are indented here.

In order to refer to a single character of LINE a substring must be used. LINE(IBEGIN:IBEGIN) must be compared with each of the punctuation characters. If one matches, control passes to statement 50. CONTINUE means 'do nothing'; the statement is merely a hook on which to hang label 50 to terminate the DO-loop. If no punctuation character matches, control passes to label 60, with IBEGIN pointing to the start of the word. If the loop ending with label 50 terminates, this must be because the scan has gone beyond LINE(80) without finding a non-punctuation character. There are no more words on the record, so control returns to label 10 to read again.

```
C SKIP TO A PUNCTUATION MARK
60    DO 70 IFIN = IBEGIN+1, 80
         DO 70 I = 1, NPUNC
70          IF (LINE(IFIN:IFIN) .EQ. PUNC(I)) GO TO 80
      IFIN = 81
80    IFIN = IFIN - 1
```

IFIN starts off one place to the right of IBEGIN, looking for the first punctuation mark after the word. If one is found, statement 80 reduces IFIN by one, since IFIN indicates the first character after the word, and what is needed is the last character of the word. What about the statement immediately after the one labelled 70? If the DO-loop ending at 70 does not find a punctuation mark anywhere, the end of the record marks the end of the word. In this case IFIN is set to 81 so that after it is decremented IFIN will correctly point to character 80. (According to the rules of Fortran 77, if the loop terminates, IFIN will have the value 81, but the extra assignment does no harm and makes the situation clear and explicit.)

Having identified the start and end of the word, it is now necessary to match the word within LINE with those stored in CH.

```
C IDENTIFY THE WORD
        DO 90 I = 1, NWDS
 90     IF (CH(START(I):TERM(I)) .EQ. LINE(IBEGIN:IFIN))
      + GO TO 120
```

Statement 90 has been continued on to a second line. This is done by means of a character (any character except blank or zero) in the sixth position of the continuation line.

If we try all the words in CH and fail to find a match, the new word must be stored. This can only happen if there is room, both for the characters and for a new word.

```
C ADD NEW WORD
        IF (NWDS .EQ.WDMAX) THEN
          WRITE (*, 100)
 100      FORMAT (' *** TOO MANY WORDS ***')
          GO TO 30
        ENDIF
        LENGTH = IFIN - IBEGIN + 1
        IF (NCH + LENGTH .GT. MAXCH) THEN
          WRITE (*,110)
 110      FORMAT (' *** TOO MANY CHARACTERS ***')
          GO TO 30
        ENDIF
        NWDS = NWDS +1
        START(NWDS) = NCH + 1
        TERM(NWDS) = NCH + LENGTH
        NCH = NCH + LENGTH
        CH(START(NWDS):TERM(NWDS)) = LINE(IBEGIN:IFIN)
        COUNT(NWDS) = 1
        GO TO 30
```

An IF statement may have only one statement as its trailer (eg statement 90 above) or it may (as here) have a sequence of statements bracketed by THEN and ENDIF.

If a match was found, all that is needed is to increment the count of this word and to return to skip punctuations once more.

```
120    COUNT(I)* = COUNT(I) + 1
       GO TO 30
```

All that remains now is to supply the code to print out the results when all input records have been processed.

```
C PRINT THE RESULTS
130    DO 140 I = 1, NWRDS
140        WRITE (*,150) COUNT(I), CH(START(I):TERM(I))
150    FORMAT (' ', I5, A20)
       END
```

Format 150 assumes that no word will be longer than 20 characters. Because we are writing out a substring of CH, only a single specification can be given in the format. The format specification A20 will cause the word to be printed out right adjusted within a field of 20 positions. Short words will appear far from their corresponding counts. Words too long to be printed will be truncated. This is yet another aspect of the failure to support variable length character strings.

A better result is obtained if we do not write out the word as a single substring, but rather write out each character of the word. If more than enough format specifications are provided, the longest word will be printed, and all words will be left adjusted next to their frequency counts. The final part of the program then becomes:

```
C PRINT THE RESULTS
130    DO 140 I = 1, NWRDS
140        WRITE (*,150) COUNT(I),
     +         (CH(J:J), J = START(I), TERM(I))
150    FORMAT (' ', I5, ' ', 80A1)
       END
```

The continuation of statement 140 here contains a kind of DO-loop. Such a loop within a WRITE statement is known as an implied-DO. The integer variable J is used as a counter. The effect is that the substring CH(J:J) is selected repeatedly, with J taking all values from START(I) to TERM(I). In this way the whole word is printed character by character.

11.3   Pascal

Pascal is not able to compare or move substrings as Fortran 77 can, so these operations must be done character by character. Reading and writing must also be done a character at a time. Apart from such details, it would be possible to translate the Fortran 77 program above directly into a Pascal program. However, it will be more instructive to implement a somewhat different method in order to show some of the variations which are possible.

The Fortran 77 program used two computer words to hold the start and end of each English word. The Pascal version will only store the length of the word - a single quantity. Moreover, the length of a word will not be a very large number. It is possible to store such a number in a single byte. Even a 6-bit byte will allow words up to 63 characters in length, and for 8-bit bytes the limit is 255. If (and it is a very big 'if') no word will be found too frequently, the count for each word may also be kept in one byte. This implies that the data will be quite brief. In English about 10% of running text consists of the word 'the', for instance. But just for the sake of the example, let us suppose that our word counts do not overflow.

Now we have removed the need for three of the four major vectors. Counts, lengths and characters can be placed in one array, which we will call vec. A word now exhibits the following data structure:

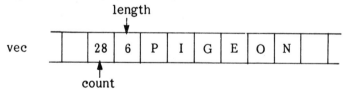

When matching a new word with those already stored, we take the value in the second byte as the length ($\underline{n}$). If the strip from the third byte to byte $\underline{n}$+2 does not match the new word, we can leapfrog over this word to the next, whose data structure starts $\underline{n}$+2 bytes further on.

An advantage now accrues which may not be immediately apparent. In the Fortran 77 program it was necessary to estimate beforehand how many words might be encountered (MAXWD) and how many characters in total they might occupy (MAXCH). If one of these commodities was amply provided the program might

110

nevertheless fail because the other one ran short. In the revised structure we only need one commodity - the vector vec. We may increase the size of this until all available store is utilised, without having to make an agonising judgment concerning how to divide the store between competing claims.

Another trick of the trade now emerges. In the Fortran 77 version we compared words of unequal length, relying on the shorter word being in effect padded out with blanks. Pascal requires us to compare character by character, so it is necessary to test the two lengths first. We only need to test for equality, so if the lengths differ no characters need be compared. The way we now intend to store the words is a great help here. The length can be considered to be an extra character preceding the word. When two words are compared, the comparison starts with the length bytes. If the lengths are different, the comparison stops at that point. If the lengths are the same, the comparison continues with the characters of the words.

One other modification may be introduced. In the Fortran 77 version the new word was compared with all words already stored. If all words had been tested unsuccessfully, the new word was stored. Another possibility, which will be followed here, is to store the new word at the outset. Then the comparison loop is sure to match. If a match is found on any but the recently stored word, the space occupied by the latter is freed once more.

Now we are in a position to start writing the Pascal program. The program statement and declarations come first.

```
program words (input, output);
const    maxbytes = 7000;
         maxwordlength = 80;
         npunc = 5;
var      vec: array [1 .. maxbytes] of char;
         word: array [1 .. maxwordlength] of char;
         punc: array [1 .. npunc] of char;
         ch: char;
         wordlength, nextfree: integer;
         letter: Boolean;
```

The program statement gives warning that reading and writing will be performed from the default input and output streams. Constants are declared for the limit on the vector of bytes, the longest possible word and the number of punctuation characters. A single character variable ch is reserved for reading and writing. The integer variable wordlength will be used for the length of word assembled from the input. The variable nextfree is used to show the next unused location within vec. Boolean values may have **true** or **false** values. The variable letter is **true** if the last character read from the input was a letter.

This is now the place to define any procedures which will be called. The main or top-level program then comes last. This ordering does not enable us to see the top-down structuring of the program very well, so the components will be introduced in a non-Pascal order here.

Although it is not essential to have procedures in this program, the structure of the program is more simply displayed by modularising. The top-level program then looks like this.

```
begin
  nextfree := 1;
  punc[1] := ' ';          punc[2] := '.';
  punc[3] := ',';          punc[4] := '(';
  punc[5] := ')';
  while not eof do
    begin
      getword;
      if wordlength > 0 then identify
    end;
  listwords
end.
```

The first few statements initialise the pointer for vec and the punctuation characters. Then there follows a loop which will continue until the function eof returns a value of **true** signalling that end of file has been encountered on the standard input. Within this loop calls are made first to procedure getword which assembles a word from the input, and then, if a word has been found, to procedure identify which will perform the comparisons and increment the frequency count. When this loop terminates, procedure listwords is called to print out the words and their counts.

Now procedure getword must be presented.

```
procedure getword;
begin
  skippunc;
  wordlength := 0;
  if not eof then
    begin
      skiptopunc;
      storeword
    end
end;
```

This procedure first calls procedure skippunc (which skips over punctuation in the input). It then initialises the length of the input word to zero. Unless end of file has been encountered, procedure skiptopunc is called to scan non-punctuation characters, assembling a word, and then storeword is called to transfer this word to vec.

Now the procedures used within getword will be defined, starting with skippunc.

```
procedure skippunc;
var     i: integer;
begin
  repeat
    read(ch);
    letter := true;
    for i := 1 to npunc do
      if ch = punc[i] then letter := false
  until letter or eof
end;
```

A local integer variable i is declared for use as a counter. The procedure consists of one loop, repeating the statements until either a non-punctuation is found, or the end of file. A character is read within the loop and compared with all the punctuation characters.

Now here is another procedure called from getword.

```
procedure skiptopunc;
var     i: integer;
begin
  repeat
    wordlength := wordlength + 1;
    word[wordlength] := ch;
    read(ch);
    for i := 1 to npunc do
      if ch = punc[i] then letter := false
  until  (not letter) or eof
end;
```

On entry to this procedure letter is **true** and ch contains the first letter of a word. The loop stores a character in the vector called word, reads another character and tests whether this is a punctuation character.

Here is the third and last of the procedures called from getword.

```
procedure storeword;
var     i: integer;
begin
  if nextfree + wordlength + 1 > maxbytes then
    begin
      write('No room for ');
      for i := 1 to wordlength do write(word[i]);
      writeln;
      wordlength := 0
    end
  else
    begin
      vec[nextfree] := chr(0);
      vec[nextfree+1] := chr(wordlength);
      for i := 1 to wordlength do
        vec[nextfree+i+1] := word[i]
    end
end;
```

If there is not enough room in vec to store the newly assembled word, a diagnostic is printed out and the wordlength is set to zero to indicate that there is no word to be identified. Otherwise, the word is copied into vec, the word count being set to zero initially, so that when the word is identified and its count incremented, the count will end up correctly as one. Because an integer value is being put into a character location, the Pascal function chr is needed. This applies both to the frequency count and to the word length.

Having defined procedure getword and its three descendants, we can now define another of the procedures called by the top-level program.

```
procedure identify;
var     k, next, length: integer;
        match: Boolean;
begin
    next := 1;
    repeat
        match := true;
        for k := 1 to ord(vec[next+1]) + 1 do
            if vec[k+next] <> vec[k+nextfree] then match := false;
        if not match then next := next + ord(vec[next+1]) + 2
    until match;
    vec[next] := chr(ord(vec[next]) + 1);
    if next = nextfree then nextfree := next + wordlength + 2
end;
```

The variable next always points to the start of the next word's data structure within vec. The variable nextfree points to the start of the new word's data structure. The two words are compared, starting with the two lengths. Then next leapfrogs over the current word to the next one. When a match is found (as found it surely will be), the appropriate count is incremented. If the matching word is in fact the new word, then the pointer to the next free byte within vec is moved over this word.

Note that the function ord must be used to convert a byte within vec to the corresponding integer value, and the function chr for the reverse process.

Finally the last procedure directly called from the top-level code is to be presented.

```
procedure listwords;
var     i, k: integer;
begin
  i := 1;
  while i < nextfree do
    begin
      write(ord(vec[i]), ' ');
      for k := 1 to ord(vec[i+1]) do write(vec[i+k+1]);
      writeln;
      i := ord(vec[i+1]) + 2
    end
end;
```

The parts of the Pascal program have been presented here in the most suitable order for understanding their relationships. They should be assembled in the following order to please the Pascal compiler.

- declarations
- procedure skippunc
- procedure skiptopunc
- procedure storeword
- procedure getword
- procedure identify
- procedure listwords
- top-level code.

11.4   SNOBOL

As might be expected, the SNOBOL program is very much shorter and we do not have to spend much time considering what data structures to use. A table will be defined, the words being used as subscripts and each value being the number of times that word has appeared. Initialisation statements are used to define the table, the punctuation marks and the pattern.

```
COUNT = TABLE()
PUNC  = ' .,()'
PAT  =  BREAK(PUNC) . WORD  SPAN(PUNC)
```

This pattern will work correctly when the next word is at the start of the string. The first word of the string will be assigned to WORD, and all punctuation characters immediately following the word will be matched also.

```
* READ RECORDS AND STRIP OFF WORDS
READ  LINE  =  INPUT  ' '                          :F(WRITE)
      LINE  POS(0)  SPAN(PUNC)  =
TAKE  LINE  PAT  =                                 :F(READ)
      COUNT<WORD> = COUNT<WORD> + 1    :(TAKE)
```

In case a word ends at the end of a record, a blank is appended to each record as it is read. Then all punctuation is removed from the start of LINE so that the first word is at the start of the string. A loop then strips each word from LINE and increments the appropriate count.

```
* PRINT OUT RESULTS
WRITE LIST  =  CONVERT(COUNT,'ARRAY')
      I  =  1
PUT   OUTPUT = LIST<I,2> ' ' LIST<I,1>            :F(END)
      I  =  I + 1                                 :(PUT)
END
```

The table COUNT is converted to an array called LIST. A loop prints out the counts and the words, failing when the index I goes out of range.

11.5 Searching for strings

The sample programs given in this chapter all had to face the same common problem. Given a list of strings already stored, when a new string is encountered, how can we find whether it matches one of the old strings? This is the problem of searching for a given string.

The Fortran 77 and Pascal programs used a linear search. The words were all stored in sequence, and the new string compared with each one in turn. When n strings have been stored, n comparisons are needed to discover that a word has not been encountered before, and on average n/2 comparisons to identify a word already stored.

There are ways of greatly improving the efficiency of such a search. One method which can be used is the binary search. Let us suppose that the words are stored in alphabetical order. Then the first comparison will be between the new word and the word stored in the middle of the list. If the search is identical, the search is at an end. If the newcomer precedes the central word alphabetically, the first half of the list of words is selected; if it follows, the second half is selected. Now the same procedure is followed once more, but with a list which is half the size. Each comparison either succeeds or halves the size of the test list. The number of comparisons needed in this case is of the order of $\log_2 n$. If n is 1024, $\log_2 n$ is 10, so this method is far more efficient than a linear search.

One problem with the binary search is the need for the items to be kept in order. When a new item is to be added, this may involve moving many items to new positions. One way out of this problem is to store pointers to the items in a binary branching tree. It does not matter where the words are stored or in what order. When a new word is encountered a pointer to it is appended at the appropriate place in the tree. For a description of this process in a slightly different context see Day (1972) pp. 76ff. A full description of binary search is given in Knuth (1973) pp. 406ff.

A method which can be faster than binary search is that of hashing. A simple introduction to this is given in Day (1972) pp. 37ff. For a thorough treatment see Knuth (1973) pp. 506ff.

In its simplest terms, the method works as follows. A table is reserved with more space than is needed to store (pointers to) all the words. A new word is 'hashed' by distilling from the word an integer value suitable for use as an index to the table. If the (pointer to) an identical word is stored at that location in the table, then a match has been found. If the location is empty, then (a pointer to) the new word may be stored there.

All goes well until two words are found which hash to the same location. This is called a 'collision', and various strategies have been proposed for resolving the situation. The simplest of these is to step cyclically through the table from the point of collision until a matching word or an empty location is found.

The hashing function needs to be selected carefully. The results for a random selection of input data should preferably be evenly distributed within the table. When the input consists of words of varying lengths, how does one design a suitable hashing function? The answer appears to be 'by trial and error'. Two machine-dependent examples are given in Griswold (1972) pp. 191-3 and 214-16, describing how SNOBOL hashing is implemented on IBM and CDC machines.

The consequence of the previous sentence should not be missed. All strings (both identifiers and values) in a SNOBOL program are hashed into the string store for rapid identification.

One further method of storing and matching strings should be mentioned here. This consists of storing all the words in a special tree, called a 'trie' in Knuth (1973) pp. 481ff. If the words are made up only of capital letters then each node of the tree will have 26-way branches. A tree containing the words AND, ANT, ARE, ART, ON and OR may be represented as

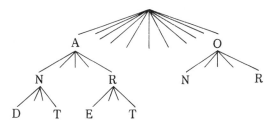

When matching a new word against the tree, each letter is taken in turn and is used to select the appropriate branch. Extra flags need to be inserted in the tree to indicate the end of a word which forms part of a longer word. For example, if the word AN were to be inserted into the tree above, the leftmost N (under the A) would need such a flag.

12

Concordance production

12.1   The problem

There are various possible forms for a concordance. Some take the same form as the index used as an example in section 10.4, ie a list of words, each one followed by a series of references. This form is sometimes referred to as a 'keyword out of context' or 'KWOC' concordance, as no context is given for the keyword.

The form of concordance to be demonstrated here is the 'keyword in context' or 'KWIC' concordance. Each line of the output has a word centralised within as much context as possible, with the reference of the line on which this word appeared in the input.

In order to keep the examples here of practical length, the problem and its solution will be as simple as possible. The references will be the line numbers of the input records. The context used will not go beyond the line in which the word appears. The concordance lines will not be sorted; rather, it is to be expected that the output will be passed through a sort/merge program so that output lines with the same keyword will be sorted together.

As an example of the kind of output to be expected, let us suppose that the input records are as follows:

and everywhere that Mary went
the lamb was sure to go.

One output line will be produced for every word in the input. The output lines will be:

<pre>
                       and everywhere that Mary   1
                   and everywhere that Mary went   1
               and everywhere that Mary went   1
           and everywhere that Mary went   1
       verywhere that Mary went   1
                           the lamb was sure to go   2
                       the lamb was sure to go   2
                   the lamb was sure to go   2
               the lamb was sure to go   2
           the lamb was sure to go   2
       he lamb was sure to go   2
</pre>

When these lines have been sorted the familiar KWIC concordance
will result:

<pre>
                       and everywhere that Mary   1
                   and everywhere that Mary went   1
       he lamb was sure to go   2
                       the lamb was sure to go   2
           and everywhere that Mary went   1
               the lamb was sure to go   2
           and everywhere that Mary went   1
                           the lamb was sure to go   2
           the lamb was sure to go   2
                   the lamb was sure to go   2
       verywhere that Mary went   1
</pre>

The method to be followed will be the same in all three
languages. The line read in will be surrounded by enough blanks
to ensure adequate context for both the first and the last word.
Starting from the beginning of the line, the start of each word
will be found in turn. Once the start of a word is found, an
output line is generated.

The start of a word is found by skipping any non-punctuation
characters belonging to the previous word, then skipping
punctuation characters to the first character of the next word.

An output line is generated as follows. From the start of the
next word, a pointer is moved back over the preceding context.
From the pointer's position, a full line of characters is printed
out, followed by the number of the input line. The situation may
be represented diagrammatically as follows:

start of word

blanks ↓ blanks

and everywhere that Mary went

The ruler represents the line to be output. The ruler is moved along until the arrow on it lines up with the start of the next word. All characters alongside the ruler are then printed.

The questions remaining are then (a) how long is the ruler, and (b) where is the arrow on it? This is to ask (a) how many characters of word + context are required for an output line, and (b) how many characters of preceding text are required? Provided that each word is approximately centred in its context and that the line (including the line number) is not too long for the printer, these numbers are fairly arbitrary. Here we will choose a line 90 characters long, with the word occurring at position 42. This means that at least 41 blanks are needed before the line read in, in case the latter has a word at the very beginning of it. If the line has a one-letter word at the very end, 48 blanks should follow. If 80-character records are read, the total length of the buffer should be at least 169 characters.

12.2   Fortran 77

Once again, the program will be presented interspersed with description.

```
CHARACTER LINE(169), PUNC(5)
DATA LINE /169 * ' '/, PUNC /' ', '.', ',', '(', ')'/
DATA LINO /0/
```

The buffer LINE is initialised to blanks by means of the DATA statement, and PUNC is set to contain the punctuation characters. The variable LINO will be used to hold the input line number. It is initialised to zero, and will be incremented every time a line is read in.

122

```
10   READ (*, 20, END=110) (LINE(I), I=42, 121)
20   FORMAT (80A1)
     LINO = LINO + 1
     MARK = 40
```

The READ statement here incorporates an implied-DO. The variable I is used as a counter as well as the subscript for LINE. A total of 80 characters are read in and placed in LINE(42), LINE(43), ... LINE(121). This reads a complete input line and places it in the correct position within its margins of blanks. The input line number is incremented. A pointer within LINE is initialised so that the start of the first word will be correctly found by the next two sections of the program.

```
C SKIP REST OF CURRENT WORD
30   DO 50 MARK = MARK + 1, 121
     DO 40 I = 1, 5
40   IF (LINE(MARK) .EQ. PUNC(I)) GO TO 60
50   CONTINUE
     GO TO 10
```

MARK will be set to point to the first character of each word. Starting from the character after this one, a scan is made until a punctuation character is found. If LINE(121) is reached and still no punctuation character is found, the previous word must have extended to the end of the line. Control then returns to read another line. If a punctuation is found, control passes to the next section.

```
C SKIP PUNCTUATION
60   DO 80 MARK = MARK + 1, 121
     DO 70 I = 1, 5
70   IF (LINE(MARK) .EQ. PUNC(I)) GO TO 80
     GO TO 90
80   CONTINUE
     GO TO 10
```

When this section is entered, LINE(MARK) contains a punctuation character. Starting from the next character, all further punctuation characters are skipped. If all characters up to and including LINE(121) are found to be punctuation characters, the line read in contains no more words and so control returns to read in another line. If a character is encountered which does not match any of the punctuations, control passes to the next section.

```
C OUTPUT LINE WITH CENTRED WORD
   90   WRITE (*, 100) (LINE(I), I = MARK-41, MARK+48), LINO
  100   FORMAT (' ', 90A1, I5)
        GO TO 30
  110   END
```

Finally, when MARK points to the start of the next word, a line with this word in the centre of it is written out. Then control returns to skip the rest of this word to find the start of the next.

12.3   Pascal

This time the Pascal program will be presented without any procedures. As almost the whole program consists of a single loop, the complete program will be shown as a unit on the next page.

The array called buff is used as the buffer. Two integers are used to hold indices with this array; linept points to the last character read from the input record, and charpt points to the character currently under examination. The Boolean notpunc is used to record whether buff[charpt] is a punctuation character or not.

The punc array is initialised to the punctuation characters. The first 41 elements of buff are filled with blanks. The line number (lino) for input records is set to zero. Then the main loop begins, terminated only when end of file is found.

A full line of characters is read into buff, starting from position 42. Function readln is then called to skip past the end of line. The line number is incremented. A further 48 blanks are added to buff to serve as the right margin. Then charpt is set to 40 (pointing within the left margin) before the loop which finds word beginnings.

A search is made for a non-punctuation character. If one is found, notpunc is set to **true,** which causes the inner loop to terminate. It also terminates when all the characters read in have been processed without a further non-punctuation being found, in which case notpunc is **false.**

If notpunc is **true,** an output line is generated. The start of a new word is at buff[charpt], so a strip of buff is printed starting 41 characters before this and ending 48 characters after it.

```pascal
program concord (input, output);
const   npunc = 5;
var     buff: array [1 .. 169] of char;
        punc: array [1 .. npunc] of char;
        lino, linept, charpt, i: integer;
        notpunc: Boolean;
begin
  punc[1] := ' ';    punc[2] := ',';      punc[3] := '.';
  punc[4] := '(';    punc[5] := ')';
  for i := 1 to 41 do buff[i] := ' ';
  lino := 0;
  while not eof do
    begin
      linept := 41;
      while not eoln do
        begin
          linept := linept + 1;
          read(buff[linept])
        end;
      readln;
      lino := lino + 1;
      for i := linept+1 to linept+48 do buff[i] := ' ';
      charpt := 40;
      repeat
        repeat
          charpt := charpt + 1;
          notpunc := true;
          for i := 1 to npunc do
            if buff[charpt] = punc[i] then notpunc := false;
        until (charpt > linept) or notpunc;
        if notpunc then
          begin
            for i := charpt-41 to charpt+48 do write(buff[i]);
            writeln(l          end;
        while notpunc do
          begin
            charpt := charpt + 1;
            for i := 1 to npunc do
              if buff[charpt] = punc[i] then notpunc := false
          end
      until charpt > linept
    end
end.
```

125

Finally lino is appended to the line by means of a call to writeln, which also terminates the output line.

Non-punctuation characters constituting the remainder of this word are then skipped over, using notpunc to indicate when a punctuation is eventually found.

This whole process (skipping punctuations, printing a line, skipping to a punctuation) is repeated until all the characters read in from the input line have been examined.

12.4 SNOBOL

The SNOBOL program is so short it can be presented in one piece.

```
        PUNC = ' .,()'
        SKIPWORD = BREAK(PUNC) SPAN(PUNC)
        LINO = 0
READ    LINE = DUPL(' ',41) INPUT DUPL(' ',48)      :F(END)
        LINO = LINO + 1
        LINE SPAN(PUNC) @POSN                        :F(READ)
NEXT    LINE LEN(POSN - 41) LEN(90) . OUTLINE        :F(READ)
        OUTPUT = OUTLINE LINO
        LINE LEN(POSN) SKIPWORD @POSN                :(NEXT)
END
```

The first three lines are initialisation, storing punctuations, setting up a pattern which will skip from one word to immediately before the next, and initialising the line number to zero. (The last of this is not strictly necessary, since LINO would originally have the null string as its value, which converts to zero in a numeric context.)

The line READ takes an input record and fits blank margins around it. The line number is incremented. Then all punctuations are skipped from the start of the buffer. The cursor position immediately before the first word is placed in POSN. Line NEXT moves back 41 characters from this position, and assigns the following 90 characters to OUTLINE. This is then written out, together with LINO. The last line before END skips over the word and the punctuation characters after it. It does so by starting POSN characters along the buffer, applying the pattern stored in SKIPWORD and leaving the cursor position before the next word in POSN once more. Control then passes to NEXT to get the new concordance line out of the buffer. After the last word has been skipped over, POSN will be moved beyond all the punctuation which follows it, and so will be left pointing to the end of LINE. This will cause line NEXT to fail, and control to return to READ.

12.5   Extensions

The type of concordance generated by the programs in this chapter is certainly very primitive. Practical concordances cannot be limited by the restrictions imposed here. Various ways in which the programs might be extended will be considered briefly.

The context surrounding a word should not be limited to the input record in which it occurs. In this case the logic of the program must be changed considerably. In order to compress as much context as possible on to each line, when a record is read in, multiple blanks should be converted to one blank, especially trailing blanks at the end of the record. At the start of the program a left hand margin of blanks is necessary, but the right hand margin for the first record should contain the second record, and if this is not long enough, the third.

When lines have been generated for all the words in the first record, the 'ruler' needs to be moved so that its arrow is opposite words in the second record. Action needs to be taken lest the right hand end of the ruler protrudes beyond the buffer. The contents of the buffer could be moved left so that the second record occupies the space originally taken up by the first record. However, this involves copying many characters. Another solution is to consider the buffer to be circular, as in Day (1972) p. 58. New records are always added cyclically to the right of previous ones, and the ruler is now an arc of a circle, always swinging clockwise past the buffer.

The input record number is not usually the reference required by the maker of a concordance. The true reference (perhaps to a book, chapter, page and line) may be contained in a certain field of each record. This must be stored to be printed with each concordance line.

If it is necessary to read ahead in order to pack in sufficient context for each word, a record may be read which has a reference different from that belonging to the words currently in the centre of the lines being generated. This implies that a list of references needs to be kept, with pointers to the place within the buffer at which each reference becomes the current one. A little thought will show that this list of references should also be circular.

12.6   Conclusions

As the previous section demonstrates, many of the problems which arise when processing text are not really due to the nature of text at all. Rather, they involve the data structures necessary for handling logical complexities.

If the programming language gives little support for text processing, it is necessary for the programmer in addition to create the data structures needed for manipulating characters and strings, as was shown in Chapter 11. In that chapter, further complexity was avoided because the strings stored did not need deleting. A more flexible and efficient system would have been very hard to program.

The conclusion must be that some current general-purpose languages give only rudimentary help for those involved in text processing. These languages are, where character strings are concerned, little higher than machine code. What is needed very often is the ability to handle variable length character strings without constraint, and to perform powerful operations (such as pattern matching) on them. Even in an area such as concordance production, which may not be considered to need much in the way of string handling, a language like SNOBOL (for all its eccentricities of syntax) produces a program which is much shorter and easier to debug.

Moreover, a language which provides high level support for handling text has a further advantage which should not be overlooked. When programmers are freed from the burden of having to design the low level features of a text-processing system, they are not simply able to implement their algorithms more easily. They are lifted above the fog of details and able to consider algorithms which would otherwise be unthinkably complex to implement.

Perhaps in the future truly 'general-purpose' languages will shift even more from a bias towards numbers as language designers and compiler writers see the need for powerful text processing.

Solutions to exercises

Chapter 1

(1)   The forms could include some of the following:
integer
short integer
real
double precision real
packed decimal
character ('byte')
character string.

(2)

(a)   Editor, word processor, program to print text files.

(b)   Compiler, assembler.

(c)   Dis-assembler (ie a program to take the binary output from an assembler and to reconstruct source text in symbolic form).

(d)   Linkage editor, loader.

Chapter 2

(1)   Each unpacked letter is shifted left to get it into the right position, and then a bitwise 'or' operation performed to move it into the packed word.

Chapter 3

(1)   if c >= 'A' and c <= 'Z' then
             begin
                c := chr(ord(c) + 1)
                if c > 'Z' then c := 'A'
             end

(2)   i := 0
         in: read(c)
         if c = ' ' then go to out
         i := i * 10 + ord(c) - ord('0')
         go to in
         out:

(3)   i := 0
         in: read(c)
         if c = ' ' then go to out
         if c >= 'A' and c <= 'F' then
             i := i * 16 + ord(c) - ord('A') + 10
         if c >= '0' and c <= '9' then
             i := i * 16 + ord(c) - ord('0')
         go to in
         out:

Chapter 4

Exercises 1 - 3 suppose that C has been declared as a character variable.

(1)   IF (C .GE. 'A' .AND. C .LE. 'Z') THEN
             C = CHAR(ICHAR(C) + 1)
             IF (C .GT. 'Z') C = 'A'
         ENDIF

(2)   I = 0
     10 READ (*, 20) C
     20 FORMAT (A1)
         IF (C .EQ. ' ') GO TO 30
         I = I * 10 + ICHAR(C) - ICHAR('0')
         GO TO 10
     30 CONTINUE

This assumes that only blanks and numeric digits will occur. It also reads each character from a separate line!

(3)   I = 0
    10 READ (*, 20) C
    20 FORMAT (A1)
        IF (C .GE. 'A' .AND. C .LE. 'F') THEN
          I = I * 16 + ICHAR('C') - ICHAR('A') + 10
          GO TO 10
        ELSE IF (C .GE. '0' .AND. C .LE. '9') THEN
          I = I * 16 + ICHAR('C') - ICHAR('0')
          GO TO 10
        ENDIF

These statements also read one character per line. The number built up in I will be terminated by any character which is not a hexadecimal digit. It is also assumed that the letters 'A' - 'F' are adjacent in the collating sequence (which they usually are).

In exercises 4 - 6 it is assumed that c has been declared as char and i as integer.

(4)   **if** (c >= 'A') **and** (c <= 'Z') **then**
          if c = 'Z' **then** c := 'A'
          else c := succ(c);

(5)   i := 0;
        repeat
          read(c);
          if c<> ' ' **then** i := i * 10 + ord(c) - ord('0')
        until c = ' ';

(6)   i := 0;
        repeat
          read(c);
          if (c >= 'A') **and** (c <= 'F') **then**
            i := i * 16 + ord(c) - ord('A') + 10
          else if (c >= '0') **and** (c <= '9') **then**
            i := i * 16 + ord(c) - ord('0')
        until c = ' ';

Chapter 5

(1)
```
function index (string1, string2)
index := 0
if length(string1) < length(string2) then return
for index := 1 to length(string1)-length(string2)+1 do
   if substr(string1,index,length(string2)) = string2
      then return
index := 0
end
```

(2)
```
s := ""
repeat
   for i := 1 to 3 do
      begin
         dig := i - (i/10) * 10
         i := i / 10
         s := concat(itos(dig), s)
         if i = 0 then j := 3
      end
   if i > 0 then s := concat(",", s)
until i = 0
writestr(s)
```

(3)
```
procedure reverse(str)
s := ""
for i := 1 to length(str) do
   begin
      s := concat(substr(str,1,1), s)
      str := substr(str, 2, length(str))
   end
str := s
end
```

(4)
```
function select(str, i)
select := itoc(0)
if i < 1 or i > length(str) then return
select := stoc(substr(str,1,1))
end
```

Chapter 6

(1)   **type** string10 = **array** [1 .. 10] **of** char;

    ...

    procedure convert (i: integer; str: string10);
    var   j, dig: integer;
    begin
      for j := 10 **downto** 1 **do**
        begin
          dig := 1 **mod** 10;
          i := i **div** 10;
          str[j] := ch(ord('0') + dig)
        end
    end;

This procedure is crude; if the number is less than ten digits long, str will be packed with leading zeros. Perhaps the reader can do better.

(2)   **type**   str5 = **array** [1 .. 5] **of** char;
              str10 = **array** [1 .. 10] **of** char;

    ...

    function index (short: str5; long: str10): integer;
    var   i, j: integer;
              match: Boolean;
    begin
      index := 0;
      i := 0;
      repeat
        match := **true**;
        for j := 1 **to** 5 **do**
          if long[i+j] <> short[j] **then** match := **false**;
        i := i + 1
      until match **or** (i > 4);
      if match **then** index := i
    end;

(3)   The problem here is that because of the Fortran 77 restrictions on assigning substrings, a temporary variable is needed for the substring.

```
        CHARACTER*80 STRING, TEMP
        ...
        IPREV = 0
10      I = INDEX(STRING, ' ')
        IF (I .EQ. IPREV) GO TO 20
        TEMP(I:80) = STRING(I:80)
        STRING(I:80) = TEMP(I+1:80)
        IPREV = I
        GO TO 10
20      CONTINUE
```

Chapter 8

(1)
```
READ    LINE  =  INPUT                            :F(END)
        OUTPUT = LINE
        OUTPUT = LINE                             :(READ)
END
```

(2)
```
READ    LINE  =  INPUT                            :F(END)
PUSH    LINE ' ' = ' '                            :S(PUSH)
        OUTPUT  =  LINE                           :(READ)
END
```

(3)
```
IN      LINE  =  INPUT                            :F(END)
STRIP   LINE ' ' =                                :S(STRIP)
        OUTPUT  =  SIZE(LINE)                      :(IN)
END
```

(4)
```
GET     LINE  =  INPUT                            :F(END)
        SPARE  =  LINE
ZIP     SPARE ' '  =                               :S(ZIP)
        OUTPUT  =  GE(SIZE(SPARE), 5) LINE   :(GET)
END
```

134

(5)
```
NUMB  FIRST  =  INPUT                                :F(END)
SQ1   FIRST  ' '  =                                  :S(SQ1)
      SECOND  =  INPUT                               :F(END)
SQ2   SECOND  ' '  =                                 :S(SQ2)
      OUTPUT = FIRST '+' SECOND '=' FIRST + SECOND
                                                     :(NUMB)
END
```

Statements have been included (SQ1 and SQ2) to remove the blanks from FIRST and SECOND. If this were not done, these would each remain 80 characters long and would be cumbersome to print.

(6)
```
GET    LINE  =  INPUT                                :F(END)
       OUTPUT  =  LINE
PRESS  LINE  ' '  =                                  :S(PRESS)
       OUTPUT = IDENT(LINE,'END') DUPL('*',80)   :(GET)
END
```

Chapter 9

(1)
```
       RTS  =
PIP    STR  LEN(1) . CHAR  =                          :F(DONE)
       RTS  =  CHAR  RTS                              :(PIP)
DONE   STR  =  RTS
```

(2)
```
       COUNT  =  0
       PUNC  =  ' ,.():;'
       PAT  =  BREAK(PUNC) . WORD  SPAN(PUNC)
READ   LINE  =  INPUT  ' '                            :F(WRITE)
       LINE  POS(0)  SPAN(PUNC)  =
STRIP  LINE  PAT  =                                   :F(READ)
       COUNT  =  COUNT  +  1                          :(STRIP)
WRITE  OUTPUT  =  COUNT  ' words in text'
END
```

Chapter 10

(1)

```
        COUNT  =  ARRAY(20)
        PUNC  =  ' ,.():;'
        PAT  =  BREAK(PUNC) . WORD  SPAN(PUNC)
READ  LINE  =  INPUT ' '                        :F(PUT)
        LINE  POS(0)  SPAN(PUNC)  =
GET   LINE  PAT  =                               :F(READ)
        I  =  SIZE(WORD)
        COUNT<I>  =  COUNT<I>  +  1          :(GET)
PUT   I  =  0
LOOP  I  =  I  +  1
        OUTPUT = COUNT<I> ' words of length ' I  :S(LOOP)
END
```

(2)   The line between LOOP and END would be changed to:

```
        OUTPUT  =  DUPL('*', COUNT<I>)          :S(LOOP)
```

(3)

```
        LIST  =  TABLE()
        PUNC  =  ' ,.():;'
        PAT  =  BREAK(PUNC) . WORD  SPAN(PUNC)
READ  LINE  =  INPUT ' '                        :F(FIN)
        LINE  POS(0)  SPAN(PUNC)  =
GET   LINE  PAT  =                               :F(READ)
        LIST<WORD> = GT(SIZE(WORD),6)            :(GET)
FIN   LIST  =  CONVERT(LIST, 'ARRAY')
        I  =  0
LOOP  I  =  I  +  1
        OUTPUT  =  LIST<I, 1>                    :S(LOOP)
END
```

Bibliography

Balfour, A. and Marwick, D. H. Programming in Standard Fortran 77. Heinemann Educational Books, 1979.

BSI. The United Kingdom 7-bit Data Code (ISO-7-UK). BS 4730:1974. British Standards Institution, 1974.

BSI. Computer Programming Language Pascal. BS 6192:1982. British Standards Institution, 1982.

Day, A. C. Fortran Techniques. Cambridge University Press, 1972.

Griswold, R. E. The Macro Implementation of SNOBOL4. W. H. Freeman and Company, 1972.

Griswold, R. E., Poage, J. F. and Polonsky, I. P. The SNOBOL4 Programming Language (second edition). Prentice-Hall, 1971.

Jensen, K. and Wirth, N. PASCAL: User Manual and Report. Springer-Verlag, 1978.

Knuth, D. E. The Art of Computer Programming: Fundamental Algorithms (Vol. 1). Addison-Wesley, 1968.

Knuth, D. E. The Art of Computer Programming: Sorting and Searching (Vol. 3). Addison-Wesley, 1973.

Page, E. S. and Wilson, L. B. Information Representation and Manipulation in a Computer. Cambridge University Press, 1978.

Index